# LEGACY ORGANIZER
## List of Forms & Pages

### HOUSEHOLD & FAMILY MATTERS
| | |
|---|---|
| Over 100 Family Questions | *1-4* |
| Family Tree | *5-7* |
| Special Days, Birthdays, Anniversaries | *8* |
| List of Advisors & Service Professionals | *9* |
| Seasonal Household To Do Checklist | *10* |
| Documents Checklist | *11* |
| Important Household Items | *12* |

### FINANCIAL MATTERS
| | |
|---|---|
| List of Accounts | *13* |
| Income Sources | *14* |
| Lifestyle Expenses | *15* |
| Liabilities and Debts | *16* |
| Assets and Possessions | *17* |
| Christian and Charitable Giving | *18* |

### RETIREMENT AND MEDICAL MATTERS
| | |
|---|---|
| List of Internet Resources for Retirees | *19* |
| Family Medical Information | *20* |
| Medical & End-of-this-Life Decisions | *21* |

### END-OF-LIFE PLANNING MATTERS
| | |
|---|---|
| Most Important Spiritual Decision | *22* |
| Personal Information and Funeral Plans *(Man) (Woman)* | *23-24* |
| Distribution of Special Personal Possessions | *25* |
| Equitable Distribution of Family Possessions | *26* |
| People and Groups to Notify About My Homegoing | *27* |
| 40+ Things to Do After a Loved One Dies | *28* |

### ESTATE PLANNING MATTERS
| | |
|---|---|
| Top 10 Estate Planning Mistakes | *29* |
| Top 5 Ways to Get Your House in Order | *30* |
| 9 Biblical Insights for End-of This Life Planning | *31-32* |
| Guardian Choices for Children | *33* |
| How to Conduct a Family Meeting | *34* |
| Estate Planning Tools for Effective Charitable Giving | *35-36* |

### ADDITIONAL RESOURCES
| | |
|---|---|
| Additional Resources | *37* |
| Products and Resources by Dr. Brian Kluth | *38* |
| Ordering Information | *39* |
| Tips for Effectively Using the Legacy Organizer | *40* |

## RECOMMENDATION:

In order for you and your loved ones to gain the greatest benefit from any of the forms and lists in this LEGACY ORGANIZER, it will probably be best to *set aside a specific 30-90 minute time period each week* to work on this over the coming months.

Also remember to write things in PENCIL, so you can easily erase and update information as things change.

NOTE: You also have the option of ordering an electronic Microsoft Word version and an Adobe PDF file so you can easily print, modify, or customize any of the forms and lists in the LEGACY ORGANIZER. See page 49 for ordering information or go to www.MyFamilyForms.org.

# OVER 100 FAMILY QUESTIONS
## Ask or answer these family history and legacy questions

What is a legacy? A legacy by definition is something you "hand down or pass along" to others. When it comes to end-of-this-life issues, many people focus on handing down money and possessions but miss out on handing down a legacy of their life to their children, grandchildren, and/or loved ones. The truth is the money will soon be spent or redirected, and the amount given will be forgotten. What will be remembered most is your living legacy of lessons learned, loving counsel, and laughter springing from past memories that you share in stories, writings, or recordings.

The Bible speaks about passing along life legacies and our spiritual heritage to our families:
- **Proverbs 13:22** A good man leaves an inheritance (legacy) for his children's children.
- **Psalm 71:18** Even when I am old and gray, do not forsake me, O God, till I declare your power to the next generation, your might to all who are to come.
- **Psalm 78:2-4** I will open my mouth in parables, I will utter hidden things, things from of old–what we have heard and known, what our fathers have told us. We will not hide them from their children; we will tell the next generation the praiseworthy deeds of the LORD, his power, and the wonders he has done.

### RECOMMENDATIONS:

**YOUNGER FAMILIES:** Let your children look through the list and take turns asking any question they want to ask you. This would be especially good for conversations around the dinner table, in the car, or during family travels, vacations, and trips.

**ADULT CHILDREN WITH AGING PARENTS:** Look through the list and highlight some items you can use as conversation starters at holiday or family gatherings. If possible, have a recorder or videotape running. Or you can also ask a few questions each time you call to talk on the phone.

**PARENTS OR GRANDPARENTS:** You may want to write out, record (audio or videotape), email, or put on a website your answers to some of these questions and then give them to your children and grandchildren. Choose from the following list of ideas to jog your memory or to start family conversations about things you can hand down and pass along to your loved ones as part of your living legacy and spiritual heritage.

Places you've lived? Addresses, description, or location (if you can remember them)?

Names and cities of the schools you attended (grade school, middle/junior high, high school, colleges)?

Who were your best friends in school? What were they like?

What were your favorite pastimes or fun activities to do as a child?

What were some of your earliest memories about church?

What type of jobs did your parents have while you were growing up?

Did you ever move from one place to a new place? How did you feel? How did it impact your life?

What did you used to do to celebrate birthdays? Christmas? Easter? Thanksgiving? July 4th? Spring break?

What were your family finances like while you were growing up? How did that affect you?

What did your family do on the weekends? Special outings? Vacations? Where did they go for trips?

Did you ever take lessons or special classes (music, art, sports, etc.)? Did you ever collect anything?

When you were a child or a teenager, what did you want to be when you grew up?

What was a favorite school subject, school memory, or year/grade in school? Favorite teacher? Why?

How did you get to school (walk, bus, parents drive you, car pool, or…)? How far was it?

Were you ever in band, choir, club, school play or drama production, student council, sports team, etc.?

What type of grades did you have in grade school? Why? Jr. High or Middle school? High school? College?

If you played sports, what sport and position did you play? Did you ever score/win? Were you ever hurt? What were some of the biggest highlights and memories you have from being on this team?

Did you ever go to school dances or proms?

Was there ever a big tragedy among your immediate family, relatives, or friends?

Were you ever taken or called to the principal's office? Why? Did you ever go through a time of rebellion?

Special or silly talents or abilities you had growing up (or still have)?

Did you ever have any nicknames growing up? What were they? Who gave them to you?

What do you remember about the people and the neighborhood where you grew up? What did the kids do for fun in your neighborhood? What were some funny stories or people you remember?

What were experiences you had growing up camping, hunting, fishing, going on vacations, going to camp, going to summer school, being on a farm, going on retreats, being in the scouts, etc.?

Awards, trophies, records, badges, medals, scholarships, elections, or prizes you won?

What about college—if you didn't go, why not? If you did go, what was your major and why did you choose this major?

First crush? First kiss? First serious boyfriend/girlfriend? First heartbreak? First job(s)? First car?

Most funny, unique, memorable, amazing, unusual memories you have of growing up?

Names (and cities where they live or lived) of aunts, uncles, cousins, and grandparents?

What were your political affiliations, beliefs, involvements, offices, or views of voting and citizenship?

Did you have physical or medical problems as a child or in your adult life? Were you ever in a serious accident? Were you ever in a hospital?

What was the biggest event you ever attended (concert, conference, rally, game, etc.)?

The three people that have had the greatest influence on you—what did you learn from them?

Lessons learned from failures or difficulties in your life? Hardest times in your life?

Places you've traveled? Most exciting or fun things you've ever done?

Were you in any clubs, fraternities/sororities, civic groups, associations, non-profit boards, or government groups? Did you hold any leadership positions? Were you ever elected to a special office?

What was some of the best advice you ever received? Who gave it to you?

What are some of the most important lessons you learned about cars?

How or when you met your spouse? Why were you attracted to them? Details about your dating, courtship, engagement, wedding day, honeymoon, and early years before children? How did you know this was the person God had for you? Did you almost marry someone else—and if yes, what happened?

Marriage - How are you different from each other? How do these differences complement and strengthen you as people, as a couple, and as parents?

Favorite memories of your children? Most difficult, fun, or frightening experiences with your children?

Did you ever invent anything, write a book, make a musical recording, or...?

Lessons you learned along the way about money - earning, saving, giving, borrowing, investing, budgeting, gambling, credit, record keeping, paying taxes, shopping, etc.?

Lessons you learned about marriage and relationships - loving, forgiving, caring, helping, talking, or more?

Names of your sister(s), brother(s), their spouse (and where they live) and their children (and where they live)? How did you get along with your sister(s) and brother(s)?

Special attributes and abilities you see in each child and/or grandchildren? Things about them or special times when you were really proud of them?

What do you remember about how you chose each child's name?

Specific wishes and desires you have for your children and/or grandchildren?

Favorite aunt/uncle, coach, teacher, employer, friend, pastor, etc.? Why?

What are some of your favorite songs, funny songs, and hymns? If you can, sing them.

Jobs, vocations, occupations, and employers you've had over your lifetime?

What was the dumbest, bravest, most foolish, courageous, funniest, or smartest thing you ever did?

What were the circumstances or people that influenced you on your primary career path?

If you were in the military, where did you go, what was your rank, what are your most vivid memories, what did you learn, and how did you benefit from the military?

What are some funny stories from your personal life or family?

Most meaningful successes or things you have been proud of in life?

Favorite jokes and stories? Favorite recipes, meals, and desserts? Favorite pets? Favorite toys? Favorite vacation(s) or trip(s)? Favorite house? Favorite place you lived? Favorite movie(s)? Favorite bands/singers?

Encounters you have had with any famous people?

What were the major life changing events in your life?

Instruments played? If you can, record your playing.

Stories and facts you know about your parents, grandparents, aunts, uncles, cousins, or siblings?

Where were your parents or grandparents born/raised? What did they do for a living? What do you most remember about them? What was their spiritual background/heritage? What stories do you recall about them? Where are they buried (if known, provide name of town/city, cemetery, address, row #, lot #, block #, section #)?

Where (cities/towns/areas) are most of your relatives living in (sisters/brothers, cousins, aunts/uncles)?

Lessons have you learned about gambling, lying, cheating, laziness, immorality, drinking, smoking, or drugs?

Favorite hobbies, interests, activities, and sports you enjoyed in your lifetime?

Greatest tragedies or disappointments you've experienced? Greatest regrets? Greatest joys?

YOUR SPIRITUAL HERITAGE—Churches you were part of?

Circumstances and details on how you were born again?

When were you baptized?

In what ways or places have you served the Lord?

Spiritual gifts God gave you? How you used your time/abilities/gifts to serve and follow the Lord?

Stories of God's leading, provision, calling, faithfulness, forgiveness, or more?

People that most influenced you in your spiritual journey? How did they impact your life?

Things you learned and practiced about reading, studying, memorizing, and obeying the Bible?

Favorite Bible verses? Explain why these are special (or stories) about how God used these verses in your life?

How and when you came to be a generous giver? What ministries did you faithfully support? Why?

Are you assured and confident you will go to heaven when you die? What are you basing your answer on?

Other:

SPECIAL NOTE ABOUT PHOTOS: Take one evening a month and go through your family photos and write the approximate date, place, names, and connections (i.e. cousin, aunt/uncle, grandparents, etc.) of other people that may be in the photo.

# COUPLE'S FAMILY TREE

**Record the person's name and then add any of the following information:**

- **B** *(Date of birth/location)*
- **W** *(Wedding date/location)*
- **S** *(Spouse's first name/maiden name)*
- **L** *(Current location: city/town)*
- **O** *(Primary occupation/s)*
- **D** *(Date of death)*
- **C** *(Cemetary location)*
- **A** *(Adopted)*
- **H** *(Half-sibling)*
- **SS** *(Step-sibling)*

### CHILD 1:

| |
|---|
| Grandchild |
| Great Grandchildren: |
| Grandchild |
| Great Grandchildren: |
| Grandchild |
| Great Grandchildren: |

### CHILD 2:

| |
|---|
| Grandchild |
| Great Grandchildren: |
| Grandchild |
| Great Grandchildren: |
| Grandchild |
| Great Grandchildren: |

### CHILD 3:

| |
|---|
| Grandchild |
| Great Grandchildren: |
| Grandchild |
| Great Grandchildren: |
| Grandchild |
| Great Grandchildren: |

### CHILD 4:

| |
|---|
| Grandchild |
| Great Grandchildren: |
| Grandchild |
| Great Grandchildren: |
| Grandchild |
| Great Grandchildren: |

*Suggestion: If your family is larger than the spaces allowed on this form, make a photocopy of this sheet to record additional people.*

# MAN'S FAMILY TREE

**Record the people's names and then add any of the following information:**

- **B** *(Date of birth/location)*
- **W** *(Wedding date/location)*
- **S** *(Spouse's first name/maiden name)*
- **L** *(Current location: city/town)*
- **O** *(Primary occupation/s)*
- **D** *(Date of death)*
- **C** *(Cemetery location)*
- **A** *(Adopted)*
- **H** *(Half-sibling)*
- **SS** *(Step-sibling)*

| FATHER: |
|---|
| Father's Father: |
| Father's Mother: |
| Father's Sibling 1/Spouse: |
|    Children: |
| Father's Sibling 2/Spouse: |
|    Children: |
| Father's Sibling 3/Spouse: |
|    Children: |
| **MOTHER:** |
| Mother's Father: |
| Mother's Mother: |
| Mother's Sibling 1/Spouse: |
|    Children: |
| Mother's Sibling 2/Spouse: |
|    Children: |
| Mother's Sibling 3/Spouse: |
|    Children: |

| SIBLING 1/SPOUSE: | |
|---|---|
| Child 1: | Child 2: |
|    Children: |    Children: |
| Child 3 | Child 4: |
|    Children: |    Children: |
| **SIBLING 2/SPOUSE:** | |
| Child 1: | Child 2: |
|    Children: |    Children: |
| Child 3 | Child 4: |
|    Children: |    Children: |
| **SIBLING 3/SPOUSE:** | |
| Child 1: | Child 2: |
|    Children: |    Children: |
| Child 3 | Child 4: |
|    Children: |    Children: |

*Suggestion: If your family is larger than the spaces allowed on this form, make a photocopy of this sheet to record additional people.*

# WOMAN'S FAMILY TREE

**Record the people's names and then add any of the following information:**

- **B** *(Date of birth/location)*
- **W** *(Wedding date/location)*
- **S** *(Spouse's first name/maiden name)*
- **L** *(Current location: city/town)*
- **O** *(Primary occupation/s)*
- **D** *(Date of death)*
- **C** *(Cemetery location)*
- **A** *(Adopted)*
- **H** *(Half-sibling)*
- **SS** *(Step-sibling)*

| **FATHER:** |
|---|
| Father's Father: |
| Father's Mother: |
| Father's Sibling 1/Spouse: |
|     Children: |
| Father's Sibling 2/Spouse: |
|     Children: |
| Father's Sibling 3/Spouse: |
|     Children: |
| **MOTHER:** |
| Mother's Father: |
| Mother's Mother: |
| Mother's Sibling 1/Spouse: |
|     Children: |
| Mother's Sibling 2/Spouse: |
|     Children: |
| Mother's Sibling 3/Spouse: |
|     Children: |

| **SIBLING 1/SPOUSE:** ||
|---|---|
| Child 1: | Child 2: |
|     Children: |     Children: |
| Child 3 | Child 4: |
|     Children: |     Children: |
| **SIBLING 2/SPOUSE:** ||
| Child 1: | Child 2: |
|     Children: |     Children: |
| Child 3 | Child 4: |
|     Children: |     Children: |
| **SIBLING 3/SPOUSE:** ||
| Child 1: | Child 2: |
|     Children: |     Children: |
| Child 3 | Child 4: |
|     Children: |     Children: |

*Suggestion: If your family is larger than the spaces allowed on this form, make a photocopy of this sheet to record additional people.*

# SPECIAL DAYS, BIRTHDAYS & ANNIVERSARIES OF FAMILY, RELATIVES & FRIENDS

*To find out the dates for all national holidays and celebration days, go to: www.holidaysmart.com*

**B**= Birthdate  **A**= Anniversary  **D**= Death  **E**= Engagement

**JANUARY**

**FEBRUARY**

**MARCH**

**APRIL**

**MAY**

**JUNE**

**JULY**

**AUGUST**

**SEPTEMBER**

**OCTOBER**

**NOVEMBER**

**DECEMBER**

# LIST OF ADVISORS & SERVICE PROFESSIONALS

This form is important for your spouse and loved ones to have readily available when you travel or are gone.

| | Name, Company, Phone Numbers, Address or E-mail |
|---|---|
| Accountant | |
| Appliance repair | |
| Attorney | |
| Auto Insurance | |
| Baby sitter | |
| Banker | |
| Car Dealer | |
| Car Mechanic | |
| Charitable Giving | |
| Clergy | |
| Computer support | |
| Contractor | |
| Dentist | |
| Doctor for: | |
| Doctor for: | |
| Doctor for: | |
| Electrician | |
| Employee Benefits | |
| Estate Executor | |
| Exterminator | |
| Financial Advisor | |
| Handyman | |
| Heating & Air Cond | |
| Home Insurance | |
| Home Warranty | |
| Hospital | |
| Interior decorating | |
| Landscaping | |
| Lawn Care | |
| Life Insurance | |
| Med. Insurance | |
| Med. Power of Atty. | |
| Medical Clinic | |
| Pension Fund | |
| Pharmacy | |
| Plumbing | |
| Power of Attorney | |
| Snow Removal | |
| Tax Preparation | |
| Veterinarian | |
| Other: | |
| Other: | |
| Other: | |

# SEASONAL HOUSEHOLD TO DO CHECKLIST

Use this form prior to the start of each season (spring, summer, fall, winter) to help you and your spouse determine things you will do in the coming season. If you save each of the forms you fill out, this will help your spouse and loved ones know what needs to be done each season if you are gone or unable to help.

## FAMILY EVENTS

Plan, schedule, invite, decorate, purchase gifts, food, planning, shopping, get tickets, etc.

- ☐ Birthdays
- ☐ Graduations
- ☐ Weddings
- ☐ Anniversaries
- ☐ Mother's/Father's day
- ☐ Memorial weekend
- ☐ Sports events
- ☐ Family reunion
- ☐ Independence Day (July 4th)
- ☐ Vacations
- ☐ Labor day weekend
- ☐ Thanksgiving
- ☐ Christmas
- ☐ Hunting/fishing
- ☐ New Year's Day
- ☐ Super Bowl
- ☐ Coming travel/trips
- ☐ Date nights/social outings
- ☐

## SPIRITUAL

- ☐ Daily Bible devotions
- ☐ Way(s) I will serve
- ☐ Special prayer times/days
- ☐ Fellowship activities
- ☐ Bible study/Group/SS class
- ☐ Camp/conferences/retreats
- ☐ Fasting
- ☐ Outreach/service activities
- ☐ Missions trip
- ☐ Books to read or class to take
- ☐ Pastor Appreciation (Oct.)
- ☐ Scripture memory
- ☐

## CHILDREN

- ☐ Sports
- ☐ Music
- ☐ Extracurricular activities/clubs
- ☐ Camps/Retreats
- ☐ Lessons/Classes
- ☐

## VACATIONS/TRIPS

- ☐ Determine location(s)
- ☐ Flights/transportation
- ☐ Vehicle maintenance
- ☐ Passports/visas (overseas)
- ☐ Lodging plans/choices
- ☐ Activities
- ☐ People to see
- ☐ Meal plans
- ☐ Purchases for trip
- ☐

## HOUSE

Possible items to inspect, clean, fix, take out of storage, store, prepare, repair, replace or update.

- ☐ Furnace inspection
- ☐ Furnace filters
- ☐ Hot water heater
- ☐ Humidifier
- ☐ Air Conditioning
- ☐ Washer/Dryer/Vent
- ☐ Refrigerator/Freezer
- ☐ Stove/oven/range hood
- ☐ Dishwasher
- ☐ Microwave
- ☐ Test smoke detectors
- ☐ Carpets cleaned
- ☐ Flooring
- ☐ Tiled surfaces
- ☐ Gutters/downspouts
- ☐ Hose/sprinkler system
- ☐ Outdoor furniture
- ☐ Pantry – clean out old food
- ☐ Tighten cabinet knobs
- ☐ Oil hinges/locks/springs
- ☐ Thermostat/settings
- ☐ Planting/gardening
- ☐ Plumbing inspection/leaks
- ☐ Sump pump inspection
- ☐ Weather-stripping
- ☐ Gardens/flowers/plants
- ☐ Lawn fertilizer/aeration
- ☐ Lawn care/mowing
- ☐ Trees/bushes/leaves
- ☐ Roofing/overhangs
- ☐ Attic vents
- ☐ Sinks/tile caulking
- ☐ Insect/pest control
- ☐ Windows/screens
- ☐ Patio/decking/stairs/porches
- ☐ Chimney cleaning
- ☐ Firewood
- ☐ Electric sockets/lights/bulbs
- ☐ Septic tank
- ☐ Insulation
- ☐ Siding
- ☐ Fire extinguishers
- ☐ Hose/sprinkler system
- ☐ Lawn mower maintenance
- ☐ Snow blower maintenance
- ☐ Driveway
- ☐ Walks/sidewalks/paths
- ☐ Shelving/storage
- ☐ Furniture/furnishings
- ☐ Housewares/dishes
- ☐ Kitchen items
- ☐ Medical/safety supplies
- ☐ Interior/exterior painting
- ☐ Fences/gates
- ☐ Sports equipment
- ☐ Pool maintenance
- ☐ Phones/long distance service
- ☐ Computers/networks
- ☐ Electronics/TV/Cable/Internet
- ☐ Closets/drawers (discard or rotate clothing)
- ☐

## VEHICLES/ENGINES

- ☐ Inspection/tune-up
- ☐ Tires
- ☐ Routine maintenance
- ☐ Oil changes
- ☐ Brakes
- ☐ Exhaust
- ☐ Transmission
- ☐ Alignment
- ☐ License renewal
- ☐ Body work
- ☐ Motorcycle/ATV/RV/Boats
- ☐

## FINANCIAL

- ☐ Regular Christian giving
- ☐ Financial record keeping
- ☐ Year-end giving
- ☐ Tax preparation
- ☐ Because I Love You Guide
- ☐ Investment planning
- ☐ Financial goals/plans/budgets
- ☐ Training/seminars/classes
- ☐

## OTHER

- ☐ Dentist/doctor appointments
- ☐

# DOCUMENTS CHECKLIST

Gather your official, financial, and legal documents and let your spouse, key family member(s), personal representative, or executor know where they are located for easy access/retrieval.

| Documents | Physical Location of Originals (and/or name of hard drive location of computer file) | Location of copies (if applicable) or names of people who have copies with date given |
|---|---|---|
| 5 Wishes Document *(if applicable)* www.agingwithdignity.org (See page 30) | | |
| This "Legacy Organizer" manual | | |
| Automobile Titles | | |
| Birth Certificates or Adoption papers | | |
| Business Agreements | | |
| Business or Partnership Agreements | | |
| Citizenship Papers | | |
| Death Certificates | | |
| Debt/Loan Certificates | | |
| Deeds | | |
| Disability Insurance Policies | | |
| Divorce/Separation Papers *(if applicable)* | | |
| Employee Life Insurance Policies | | |
| Financial account numbers | | |
| Financial/Bank/Inv. Statements | | |
| Funeral instructions | | |
| Home & Vehicle Insurance Policies | | |
| Leases | | |
| Life Insurance Policies | | |
| Marriage Certificates | | |
| Medical Power of Attorney | | |
| Memos/Instructions about distribution of personal, sentimental, or heirloom possessions | | |
| Military Discharge Papers | | |
| Mortgages | | |
| Partnerships | | |
| Passports | | |
| Past Income Tax Returns | | |
| Personal address book | | |
| Personal Financial Statement | | |
| Power of Attorney | | |
| Pre-paid funeral arrangements | | |
| Recreational Vehicle/Equip Titles | | |
| Retirement/Pension Benefits | | |
| Social Security Cards & Benefits* | | |
| Stock Certificates/Bonds | | |
| Wills/Trusts/Estate Plans | | |
| Other: | | |
| Other: | | |

Safe Deposit Box Info *(if applicable)* – Physical Location: _____ Box Number: _____
Location of keys: _____
Name of Financial Institution: _____ Phone Number: _____
Address: _____

*Note about Social Security Benefits. The SS phone number is 1-800-772-1213. To claim SS death benefits after the death of a spouse, go to your local Social Security office and bring with you your spouse's death certificate, social security card, birth certificate, marriage certificate/license, and the birth certificates for each child.

# IMPORTANT HOUSEHOLD ITEMS

This form is important for your spouse and loved ones to have readily available when you travel or are gone.

## LOCATION OF IMPORTANT HOUSEHOLD ITEMS:

Main water turn off valve:
Hose and/or sprinkler system turn off valve:
Gas turn off valve:
Phone line junction box on the exterior of the house:
Electric circuit breakers/fuse box:
TV satellite or cable box:
Cans of paint used in interior or exterior:
Family photos:
Address book:
Owner instruction manuals for appliances/etc:
Passbooks for checkbook/saving accounts:
Cash/gold/silver/coins/precious gems:
Firearms:
Inventory or video of household items (for insurance purposes in case of fire, etc.):
Other:
Other:

## LOCATION OF KEYS OR COMBINATION LOCK NUMBERS (XX-XX-XX) OR SECURITY CODES:

Alarm/Security/Fire system:         Name of company:         Phone:
Vehicles:
Exterior house doors:         Interior house doors:
Garage:
Cabin/vacation home:
Lawn mower or yard equipment:         Snow blower:
Boat:         Boat trailer:         Motorcycle/ATV:
RV or trailer:
Gun cabinet:         Gun trigger locks:
Boat house:
Storage shed:
Location of Safe:         Key location or combination:
Location of Fireproof lock box:         Key location or combination:
Electronic entry gates:
Bicycle locks:
Television satellite or cable security codes:
Combination Lock for:         #'s:  -  -         Combination Lock for:         #'s:  -  -
Combination Lock for:         #'s:  -  -         Combination Lock for:         #'s:  -  -
Combination Lock for:         #'s:  -  -         Combination Lock for:         #'s:  -  -
Other:
Other:

## COMPUTERS

Location of computer hub:
Security code to access internet wi-fi:
Location of internet modem:
Location of computer software programs/CD's::
Location of computer hardware owner's manuals and operating CDs:
Computer #1:         Account name:         Password:
Computer #2:         Account name:         Password:
Computer #3:         Account name:         Password:
Email address:         Login:         Password:
Email address:         Login:         Password:
Email address:         Login:         Password:
Email address:         Login:         Password:
Other:
Other:

# LIST OF ACCOUNTS

*To view filled out samples, go to: www.MyFamilyForms.org*

**Provide important and confidential information for the following types of accounts:**

- **CK** *(Checking Account)*
- **SV** *(Savings Account)*
- **RF** *(Retirement/Pension Fund)*
- **ST** *(Stocks)*
- **BD** *(Bonds)*
- **CC** *(Credit Card)*
- **INV** *(Investment)*
- **MO** *(Mortgage)*
- **VP** *(Vehicle Payment)*
- **LO** *(Loans & Payments)*
- **ATM** *(ATM Card/Pin #)*
- **WS** *(Website Account)*
- **EM** *(Email Account)*
- **ON** *(Online shopping accounts—E-bay, Paypal, etc.)*
- **INS** *(Insurance—Life, Medical, House, Vehicle, Disability, etc.)*
- **CHR** *(Charitable Giving Account)*
- **FF** *(Frequent Flyer Account)*

**NOTE:** *Treat this info with the UTMOST CONFIDENCE. Only give to a spouse and/or individuals involved in your finances and estate.*

| Company and/or Account Name: | Type: | Acct #: | Phone #: | Website & Login Info: | Contact Person (if applicable): | $ Value & Date: |
|---|---|---|---|---|---|---|
| | | | | | | |

To research if your family has any unclaimed money sitting in insurance companies, banks, utility companies, stocks, etc., go to: **www.missingmoney.com**

# INCOME SOURCES

*"Honor the Lord by giving him the first part of all your income."* Proverbs 3:9
*"Everything comes from you, (Oh LORD) and we have given you only what comes from your hand."* 1 Chronicles 29:14-15

This form will help you and your spouse understand your annual income sources.
It will also help you assess how much you may want to give from your various income sources
if you want to be more faithful and generous in your Christian and charitable giving.

## Step 1
☑ Check any item that is a source of God-given cash flow or income that you normally receive over a 12 month period.

## Step 2
Determine an approximate "financial value" ($ amount) that this item represents in your life. Indicate the frequency of how often you receive these funds:

- **W** *(Weekly)*
- **B** *(Bi-weekly or 2x a month)*
- **M** *(Monthly)*
- **Q** *(Quarterly)*
- **Y** *(Yearly/annually)*
- **S** *(Sporadically)*
- **O** *(One-time amount)*

## Step 3
Indicate the percentage (%) you have prayerfully decided you will normally give to honor the Lord from whatever God-given resources He has provided for you.

| ☑ | Normal Cash & Income Over 12 Months | Amount: | Freq: | ___% = |
|---|---|---|---|---|
| ☐ | Income, wage or salary from: | | | |
| ☐ | Income, wage or salary from: | | | |
| ☐ | Income, wage or salary from: | | | |
| ☐ | Overtime pay | | | |
| ☐ | Bonuses | | | |
| ☐ | Tax returns/refunds | | | |
| ☐ | Commissions | | | |
| ☐ | Business income | | | |
| ☐ | Severance pay | | | |
| ☐ | Part-time work or moonlighting | | | |
| ☐ | Consulting fees | | | |
| ☐ | Sale of products or assets | | | |
| ☐ | Home-based business or services | | | |
| ☐ | Sale of stuff I/we own | | | |
| ☐ | Workmen's Compensation | | | |
| ☐ | Honorariums | | | |
| ☐ | Social Security | | | |
| ☐ | Pension income | | | |
| ☐ | Military pay or pension | | | |
| ☐ | Annuity | | | |
| ☐ | Union pay or pension | | | |
| ☐ | Disability income | | | |
| ☐ | Unemployment or workmen's compensation | | | |
| ☐ | Spousal or child support | | | |
| ☐ | Trust fund | | | |
| ☐ | Inheritance monies | | | |
| ☐ | Insurance settlement | | | |
| ☐ | Legal settlement | | | |
| ☐ | Income from rental or leased properties | | | |
| ☐ | Interest and/or dividends | | | |
| ☐ | Repayment of personal loans | | | |
| ☐ | Royalties from copyrights/patents | | | |
| ☐ | Rebates/Refunds/Returns/Coupons | | | |
| ☐ | Government welfare, food stamps, etc. | | | |
| ☐ | Other: | | | |
| ☐ | Other: | | | |
| **CHILDREN** *(if applicable)* | | | | |
| ☐ | Work projects | | | |
| ☐ | Allowances | | | |
| ☐ | Cash gifts *(birthday, Christmas, etc.)* | | | |
| ☐ | Part-time jobs or home business | | | |
| ☐ | Babysitting, lawn mowing, etc. | | | |
| ☐ | Other: | | | |

# LIFESTYLE EXPENSES

*Money talks: It says, "Good bye!" Where is your money going?*

**Step 1**    As best as you can, estimate how much money you are spending on a "monthly basis" in each area listed on the next page (Helpful hint: Take ANY quarterly, yearly, sometimes and one-time expenses and prorate this amount on a monthly basis).

*HELPFUL NOTE:* If you would like to find out how your spending compares to recommended national budget averages, visit: www.crown.org and click on tools and their budget guide calculator.

| AVG: | "MONTHLY AVERAGES" OF WHERE YOUR MONEY GOING AS OF ___/___/2____ |
|---|---|
| $ | **GIVING:** Church: $____ Building: $____ Needy: $____ Missions: $____ Other: $____ Other: $____ |
| $ | **HOUSING:** Rent/Mortgage: $____ Utilities: $____ Trash $____ Lawn: $____ Maintenance/Repairs: $____ Furnishing/Decorations: $____ Special Projects/Purchases: $____ Other: $____ Other: $____ |
| $ | **TELECOMMUNICATIONS:** Phone: $____ Lg Distance: $____ Cell Phone/s $____ Internet: $____ Text: $____ |
| $ | **VEHICLES:** Payments: $____ Gas: $____ Insurance: $____ Maint/Repair: $____ License: $____ Other: $____ |
| $ | **GROCERIES AND HOUSEHOLD:** Groceries: $____ Supplies: $____ Miscellaneous: $____ |
| $ | **ENTERTAINMENT/RECREATION:** Cable: $____ Videos/Movies: $____ Lessons: $____ Health Club: $____ Crafts/Hobbies: $____ Sports: $____ Events/Concerts: $____ Music: $____ Vacations: $____ Trips: $____ Camping: $____ Vacation Home: $____ Hunting/Fishing: $____ School/Scout/Civic: $____ Dinners Out: $____ Other: $____ Other: $____ Alcohol*: $____ Tobacco*: $____ Gambling*: $____ <br> *These are not recommended uses, but rather are listed to help someone determine how much money they may be spending unwisely on these items. |
| $ | **INSURANCES:** Medical: $____ Life: $____ Disability: $____ Other: $____ |
| $ | **CLOTHING:** Man: $____ Woman: $____ Children: $____ |
| $ | **MISCELLANEOUS:** Fast Food/Restaurants: $____ Meals out at work: $____ Childcare: $____ Toiletries: $____ Hair: $____ Pets: $____ Vet: $____ Subscriptions: $____ Coffee:$____ Vending Mach:$____ Other: $____ |
| $ | **GIFT GIVING & CELEBRATIONS:** Anniversaries: $____ Birthdays: $____ Weddings/Babies/Graduations: $____ Holiday Parties: $____ Children's Birthday Parties (cake/activity/favors/etc.): $____ Other: $____ |
| $ | **MEDICAL:** Doctors: $____ Hospitals: $____ Dental: $____ Prescriptions: $____ Other: $____ |
| $ | **SAVINGS/INVESTMENTS:** Savings: $____ Pension: $____ College: $____ Investment: $____ Other: $____ |
| $ | **EDUCATION:** Tuition: $____ Books: $____ Fees/Activities: $____ Room & Board: $____ Other: $____ |
| $ | **DEBTS:** Cred Cd Pymts: $____ Personal Loans: $____ Student Loans: $____ Medical Bills: $____ Other: $____ |

**Step 2**    Prayerfully review the list. Are there any items the Lord may be showing you that you could eliminate or modify to become more generous and/or to eliminate any indebtedness:
- You don't really "need" and could eliminate from your spending?
- You could meet this need more affordably by shopping around or by lowering your expectations?
- You should decrease or eliminate because you realize this expenditure is hurtful to your personal health OR to your spiritual growth and service?
- You could postpone or trust God to meet this need in another way?

**Step 3**    Based on items you identified in step 2, determine any increased amount you could give to the Lord monthly to meet a special need or giving opportunity ($_____/month for increased giving) and/or to eliminate any indebtedness ($_____/month for paying off debt).

# LIABILITIES & DEBTS

*"The borrower is servant to the lender."* Proverbs 22:7
*"The wicked borrow and do not repay, but the righteous give generously."* Psalms 37:21
*"Pay all your debts except the debt of love for others - never finish paying that!"* Romans 13:8

There are Christian classes and counselors nationwide available to help you get out of debt:
www.Crown.org • www.DaveRamsey.com • www.goodsenseministry.com
www.cheapskatemonthly.com has a great online get-out-of-debt calculator *(RPDP = Rapid Debt Repayment Plan)*

| Today's Date: ___/___/20___ | Lender | Account # | Phone # | Total Balance | Minimum Payment | % Rate |
|---|---|---|---|---|---|---|
| Sample | First Bank VISA | 3456-7891-0123-4567 | 303-555-1234 | $3211 | $125 | 18% |
| Mortgage 1 | | | | | | |
| Mortgage 2 | | | | | | |
| Home Equity | | | | | | |
| Car loan | | | | | | |
| Car loan | | | | | | |
| Furn/Appliance | | | | | | |
| Furn/Appliance | | | | | | |
| Rec Equip/Veh | | | | | | |
| Rec Equip/Veh | | | | | | |
| Electronics | | | | | | |
| Electronics | | | | | | |
| Credit Card 1 | | | | | | |
| Credit Card 2 | | | | | | |
| Credit Card 3 | | | | | | |
| Credit Card 4 | | | | | | |
| Credit Card 5 | | | | | | |
| Medical 1 | | | | | | |
| Medical 2 | | | | | | |
| Medical 3 | | | | | | |
| Medical 4 | | | | | | |
| Medical 5 | | | | | | |
| Medical 6 | | | | | | |
| Student Loan | | | | | | |
| Student Loan | | | | | | |
| Personal Loan | | | | | | |
| Personal Loan | | | | | | |
| Business Loan | | | | | | |
| Business Loan | | | | | | |
| IRS/Taxes | | | | | | |
| Other | | | | | | |
| Other | | | | | | |

**People who owe money to me/us:**

© To order the FAMILY ORGANIZER or to CUSTOMIZE THIS FORM (by ordering the Microsoft Word version), go to: www.MyFamilyForms.org

# ASSETS & POSSESSIONS

Periodically, it is wise to prayerfully consider what God has entrusted to you:
1. ☑ Determine the items (and the market or resale value) you have in your possession.
2. Prayerfully and honestly determine which of these items you need and are actually using?
3. Are there any items that could be passed along to someone you know who could benefit from their use?
4. Are there any items that should be sold?
5. Are there any items (in the near future or after your funeral) that could be given to benefit your church, a Christian ministry, or charity?

Visit www.idonate.com if you want to donate some of these assets to a church, charity or Christian organization.
**IMPORTANT NOTE:** It is wise to discuss with your charity, church, or ministry the best way to give an asset. Depending on the value and type of asset, it may be wise to have the organization assist you in obtaining the help of an experienced estate planning professional to determine how to most effectively and affordably "transfer" an asset. Careful planning with experienced professional counsel versed in evaluating tax and estate planning issues will maximize the value of this gift to a non-profit, to yourself and to your family.

*"From what you have, take an offering for the LORD. Everyone who is willing is to bring to the LORD."* Ex 35:4-5

| ☑ | List of Assets You Have In Your Possession | Estimated Value as of: _____ | Details, descriptions, or specific desires for these items. If applicable, identify any item(s) you feel God would like you to give to a ministry now or in the future *(i.e., sell the item and give the cash proceeds OR donate the specific item to a ministry to use or sell)* |
|---|---|---|---|
| ☐ | Vehicle: | | |
| ☐ | Vehicle: | | |
| ☐ | Checking Account(s) & Cash | | |
| ☐ | CD's or Savings Accounts | | |
| ☐ | Motorcycles/Recreational Vehicles | | |
| ☐ | Motor Home/RV/Trailer/Camper | | |
| ☐ | Boats/Watercraft & Equipment | | |
| ☐ | Home | | |
| ☐ | Timeshare, Condo, Vacation Property | | |
| ☐ | Sports, Exercise, Hunting Equipment | | |
| ☐ | Workshop or Garage Tools/Equipment | | |
| ☐ | Craft or Camera Equipment/Supplies | | |
| ☐ | Musical instruments | | |
| ☐ | Appliances/Furniture/Furnishings | | |
| ☐ | Jewelry or Gems or Furs | | |
| ☐ | Antiques, Art, Memorabilia or Heirlooms | | |
| ☐ | Books – Videos – Albums | | |
| ☐ | China/Crystal/Glassware/Silver/etc. | | |
| ☐ | Stocks/Bonds/Mutual funds/CDs | | |
| ☐ | US Notes/Bills/Bonds | | |
| ☐ | Commodities | | |
| ☐ | Pension Funds (Employer or Military) | | |
| ☐ | Retirement Accounts | | |
| ☐ | College Savings Funds | | |
| ☐ | Collections (Coins/Stamps/Crafts/Toys) | | |
| ☐ | Trust Fund(s) or Inheritance Funds | | |
| ☐ | Rental Properties | | |
| ☐ | Business, Farm, Ranch: Buildings/Land | | |
| ☐ | Business Vehicles/Equipment/Supplies | | |
| ☐ | Undeveloped Land or Farmland | | |
| ☐ | Livestock, Animals | | |
| ☐ | Possessions in Storage Units | | |
| ☐ | Foundation or Donor-Advised Funds | | |
| ☐ | Business Partnerships/Ownership | | |
| ☐ | Real Estate Partnerships | | |

# CHRISTIAN AND CHARITABLE GIVING

Identify: "What ministries, projects, programs, and people do you care about and want to support?"

*"You are generous because of your faith. And I am praying that you will really put your generosity to work, for in so doing you will come to an understanding of all the good things we can do for Christ."* Philemon 5-7

**Step 1** Identify the Christian ministries and charities you are currently supporting or would like to support *(see ministries list below.)*

**Step 2** After prayer, circle any existing ministry you support OR a new ministry opportunity that could best utilize your increased or sacrificial support.

**Step 3** Determine *"future"* giving priorities, amounts, or percentages you believe God wants you to give to within the next few years.

**Step 4** Determine end-of-life gifts *(percentages or amounts)* you feel God wants you to give for a select group *(specific church, ministries, or charities).*

**SUGGESTION:** If you give 10% or more to the Lord's work, consider tithing your normal expected income *(your main income source)* to your local church. Then consider giving 10% or more from all your other income sources to support other ministries and special needs.

## TYPES OF CHRISTIAN & CHARITABLE ORGANIZATIONS:

- **CHURCH**: Pastoral staff, missions, benevolence, youth, children, adult, women, men, worship, facilities, media, denomination, etc.

- **BUILDINGS & EQUIPMENT**: New facilities, relocation, expansion, renovations, vehicles, computers, program equipment, etc.

- **NEEDY**: Widows, homeless, urban ministries, crisis pregnancy, prisoners, refugees, relief, orphans, rescue missions, disabled, scholarships, etc.

- **EDUCATION**: Schools, colleges, universities, seminaries, etc.

- **SPECIAL GROUPS**: Children, women, men, families, minorities, etc.

- **MISSIONS**: Missionaries, home missions, international mission organizations, 10/40 Window, church planting, theological education, relief, leadership training and development, economic development, facilities, etc.

- **OUTREACH/DISCIPLESHIP**: Evangelism, evangelistic crusades, media, magazine, books, TV, radio, financial, campus, professional groups, sports, men, women, children, teens, camps, conference centers, etc

- **CULTURAL/ARTS/WORSHIP/MUSIC**

| Ministries & Charities You Support: | Support in the past 12 months | If desired, Special Gift within 1-5 years? | If desired, $ or % to include in will? |
|---|---|---|---|
| Your local church | | | |
| Benevolence/help for needy | | | |
| Church building project(s) | | | |

# HELPFUL INTERNET RESOURCES FOR RETIREES, AGING ADULTS AND CAREGIVERS

- *Because I Love You* **LEGACY ORGANIZER** www.MyFamilyForms.org *40 pages of valuable resources, checklists and forms for spiritual matters, finances, household information, documents, family tree, life legacy, funeral plans, wealth sharing/distribution, aging parents, child guardians, estate planning and more!*
- **Christian Retirees with RVs - Volunteer Service Opportunities** www.workersonwheels.com www.mmap.org  www.sowerministry.org  www.rvics.com  www.habitat.org/gv/rv.html
- **Christian Volunteer Opportunities for Retirees** www.servantopportunities.net  www.finishers.org
- **5 Wishes Booklet** www.agingwithdignity.org *A valuable "fill-in-the-blank" document to communicate your near-the-end-of-this-life medical, personal, emotional and spiritual wishes for family and medical staff/professionals.*
- **American Association of Retired Persons** www.aarp.org
- **Administration on Aging** www.aoa.gov
- **Solutions for Better Aging** www.agenet.org *Articles, online tools and checklists on caregiving, housing, legal, insurance, health, drugs and home.*
- **Aging Parents and Elder Care** www.aging-parents-and-elder-care.com *Excellent source for valuable articles, checklists, referrals and website links.*
- **Alzheimer's Association** www.alz.org
- **Assisted Living Info** www.assistedlivinginfo.com *Online guide for selecting an assisted living facility, retirement community, or other personal care facility anywhere in the United States.*

- **Benefits Checkup** www.benefitscheckup.org *Helps you find and enroll in federal, state, local and private programs that help pay for prescription drugs, utility bills, meals, health care and other needs.*
- **Caregiving website** www.caregiving.com
- **Center for MEDICAID and MEDICARE Services** www.cms.hhs.gov *Valuable online help and answers.*
- **Center for Medicare Advocacy** www.medicareadvocacy.org *Non-profit organization which provides education, advocacy, and legal assistance to help elders and people with disabilities obtain necessary healthcare.*
- **Children of Aging Parents Association** www.caps4caregivers.org *A nonprofit organization serving caregivers of the elderly or chronically ill with reliable information, referrals and support.*
- **Christian Association of Senior Adults** www.gocasa.org
- **Drugs.com** www.drugs.com *Comprehensive info on 24,000+ different drugs and medicines.*
- **Eldercare Locator** www.eldercare.gov
- **Family Caregiver Alliance** www.caregiver.org
- **Focus on the Family** www.family.org *Valuable articles, resources and referrals from a Christian perspective.*
- **Government Senior Citizens Resources** www.seniors.gov
- **Health Assistance Partnership** www.healthassistancepartnership.org *Information about the needs of Medicaid and Medicare beneficiaries, commercially insured consumers, and the uninsured.*
- **Mayo Clinic** www.mayoclinic.com *Health and wellness information from the Mayo clinic.*
- **Medicare** www.medicare.gov *The official US site for people with Medicare. Information about nursing homes, physicians, benefits, and coverage questions.*
- **National Alliance for Caregiving** www.caregiving.org
- **National Family Caregivers Association** www.nfcacares.org
- **Natl Assoc of Professional Geriatric Care Managers** www.caremanager.org *On-line referral service.*
- **Nursing Home Info** www.nursinghomeinfo.com *Info about choosing a nursing home, listings of facilities and a needs assessment tool.*
- **Senior Net** www.seniornet.org *Provides older adults education for and access to computer technologies.*
- **Servants on Wheels Ever Ready** www.sowerministry.org
- **Social Security Administration** www.socialsecurity.gov
- **Web MD** www.webmd.com *Online medical information and advice.*
- **Well Spouse Foundation** www.wellspouse.org *Support to partners of the chronically ill and/or disabled.*

# FAMILY MEDICAL INFORMATION

Insurance (company, policy number, phone number):
Location of insurance cards (wallet/s, desk drawer or?):
Medicaid/Medicare info:
Location of organ donor card/instructions/permissions:
Prescription/Dental/Vision:
Doctors/Dentist/Etc. (name, specialty, phone number):

## MEDICAL HISTORY
*Name of family member/relative and approximate age at time of diagnosis (if known)*

Heart disease:
Stroke:
Cancer (specific type/s):
Depression/suicide:
Diabetes:
High cholesterol:
High blood pressure:
Miscarriages:
Infant/childhood deaths:
Allergies:
Amputations (reason):
Other:
Other:

## IMMUNIZATION HISTORY
*Write names of family members and date(s) immunizations given (if known)*

Hepatitis A:
Hepatitis B:
Influenza:
MMR:
Pneumonia:
Meningitis:
Tetanus:
Chicken pox:

## MAJOR SURGERIES
*Write person's name, type of surgery, year and/or approximate age at the time of surgery (if known)*

## PRESCRIPTIONS
*Write person's name, doctor's name, name of medication, reason for medication (if known)*

# MEDICAL & END-OF-THIS-LIFE DECISIONS

One of the easiest, most effective, and most broadly-recognized resources to help you make medical and end-of-this-life decisions is a booklet called, Five Wishes®. There are over four million in print. The booklet costs $5 (or $1 each for 100 copies or more). Place orders at www.agingwithdignity.org or by calling 1-888-594-7437.

The *Five Wishes* document is one of many possible Medical Power of Attorney forms, important forms that help you express how you want to be treated if you are seriously ill and unable to speak for yourself. It is important to sign a Medical Power of Attorney that is valid in the state where you live, and that it is properly witnessed and notarized. The *Five Wishes* form is unique among living will and health agent forms because it looks to all of a person's needs: medical, personal, emotional and spiritual. It also encourages you to discuss your wishes with your family and physician.

### The Five Wishes booklet lets your family and doctors know:
1. **Who you want to make health care decisions for you when you can't make them yourself.**
2. **The kind of medical treatment you want or don't want.**
3. **How comfortable you want to be.**
4. **How you want people to treat you.**
5. **What you want your loved ones to know.**

**What is the Five Wishes booklet?** The following information is from the Five Wishes website (www.agingwithdignity.org). *Five Wishes* is an easy-to-use legal document that lets you plan in advance for how you want to be cared for in case you become seriously ill. Some people refer to it as an "advance directive" because when you complete *Five Wishes* you give direction to your doctor and family, in advance, on how you want to be treated.

- **Wish One** lets you choose the person you want to make decisions for you when you can't make them for yourself. Lawyers call it a "durable power of attorney for health care."
- **Wish Two** is a living will. It lets you put in writing the kind of medical treatment you want, or don't want, if you become seriously ill and can't communicate to anyone.
- **Wishes Three and Four** let you describe in detail how you want to be treated so that your dignity can be maintained.
- **Wish Five** gives you a chance to tell others how you want to be remembered, and express other things that might be in your heart, like forgiveness.

**Why should I fill out Five Wishes?** Without an advance directive like *Five Wishes*, you may have no control over important medical care decisions that will be made if you ever get seriously ill – such as whether to give you life-support treatment or aggressively treat your pain. Everyone has different wishes and yours won't be followed unless you make them clear. Not expressing your wishes can put your family, friends and doctor in the difficult position of guessing what kind of treatment you want, which could lead to disagreements. Completing *Five Wishes* gives you control over your care and peace of mind for you and your loved ones.

**When do I need to use Five Wishes?** The best time to fill out a document like this is *before* you face a health crisis. You never know when you are going to need *Five Wishes*, and many people put it off until it's too late. If you are over age 18, you should complete the forms now. If you are married, you and your spouse each need to fill out your own *Five Wishes* document.

**When does Five Wishes take effect?** You will always make your own health care decisions, if you are able to talk with your doctor and understand what is being said. *Five Wishes* only takes effect when you are too ill to communicate. So if you have a stroke and can't speak, or are in a coma, then your *Five Wishes* and the person you chose to be your health care agent, can help direct your care with your doctor.

**Is Five Wishes a legal document?** Yes. It was written with the help of the American Bar Association's Commission on the Legal Problems of the Elderly. It meets legal requirements under the advance directive statutes in most states.

For additional answers, or to order booklets for you or your loved ones, go to: www.agingwithdignity.org

# YOUR MOST IMPORTANT SPIRITUAL DECISION: STEPS TO PEACE WITH GOD

**THE GREATEST GIFT** you will ever be able to leave your family is to give them the assurance they know what will happen to you when you leave this world. In order to do this, you must receive the greatest gift that God willingly offers you, the free gift of eternal life. The Bible says in Romans 6:23, *"The wages of sin is death, but the **free gift** of God is **eternal life** through Christ Jesus our Lord."* Read through the rest of this page to know what you must do in order to receive this free gift and live forever with God.

### 1. God's Plan—Peace And Life
God loves you and wants you to experience His peace and life. The Bible says, **"For God so loved the world that he gave his only begotten Son, that whosoever believeth in him should not perish, but have life."** John 3:16

### 2. Our Problem
Being at peace with God is not automatic because you by nature are separated from God. The Bible says, **"For all have sinned and fall short of the glory of God."** Romans 3:23

### 3. God's Remedy—The Cross
God's love bridges the gap of separation between God and you. When Jesus Christ died on the Cross and rose from the grave, He paid the penalty for your sins. The Bible says, **"He personally carried the load of our sins in his own body when he died on the cross..."** 1 Peter 2:24

### 4. Our Response—Receive Christ
You can cross the bridge into God's family when you receive Christ by personal invitation. The Bible says, **"But as many as received Him, to them He gave the right to become children of God, even to those who believe in His name..."** John 1:12

To receive Christ you need to do four things:
1) **ADMIT** your spiritual need. "I am a sinner."
2) **REPENT** and be willing to turn from your sin.
3) **BELIEVE** that Jesus Christ died for you on the cross.
4) **RECEIVE** through prayer, Jesus Christ into your heart and life.

The Bible says (Christ is speaking), **"Behold, I stand at the door and knock; if any man hears my voice, and opens the door, I will come in..."** Revelation 3:20
**"Everyone who calls on the name of the Lord will be saved."** Romans 10:13

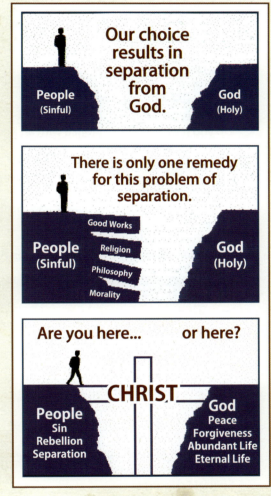

© Billy Graham Evangelistic Association
Used by permission

Here is a suggested prayer for you to pray:

*Dear Lord Jesus: Thank you for loving me. I know I am a sinner. I believe you died on the cross for my sins. Right now, I turn from my sins and open the door of my heart and life to you. I receive you as my personal Lord and Savior. Thank you for now saving me. Amen*

I want my family and loved ones to know that I have prayed to receive Christ, and I have assurance that when I leave this world I will go to heaven to be with my personal Savior, the Lord Jesus Christ.

**Man's signature:**_____ **Date:**_____

**Woman's signature:**_____ **Date:**_____

For additional spiritual encouragement by Dr. Brian Kluth, you can listen to or watch his sermons posted on www.MyFamilyForms.org

# PERSONAL INFORMATION & FUNERAL PLANS (Man)

*Use additional paper if necessary*

| | |
|---|---|
| Full Name: | Social Security Number: |
| Date of Birth *(DOB)*: | Place of Birth: |
| Driver's License State/Number: | |
| Full Name of Father: | Father's Birthplace: | Father's DOB: |
| Full Name of Mother: | Mother's Birthplace: | Mother's DOB: |
| Siblings and their current location: | |
| If married, Wedding Date: | Spouse's Maiden Name: | DOB: |
| Child #1 Name: | DOB: | Soc Sec #: | Spouse: |
| Child #2 Name: | DOB: | Soc Sec #: | Spouse: |
| Child #3 Name: | DOB: | Soc Sec #: | Spouse: |
| Child #4 Name: | DOB: | Soc Sec #: | Spouse: |
| Occupations/Position -Title/Years: | |
| Employers/Years: | |
| Do you have any life insurance with an Accidental Death Benefit *(which pays extra if you died accidentally)*? | |
| Grade School/s, Middle School/Jr. Highs/Cities: | |
| High School(s)/City/Year Graduated: | |
| College(s)/Universities/Years/Cities/Degrees/Majors: | |
| Places lived in/years: | |
| Military from _____ to _____ in the (branch): | Rank: | Serial #: | Discharge Date: |
| Places served in Military: | |
| Churches Attended/Cities/Years: | |
| Professional Groups, Civic, Clubs, Lodges, Associations: | |
| Closest friends: | |

## FUNERAL PLANNING *Provide instructions, notes, name(s), addresses, phone numbers, emails, etc.*

| | |
|---|---|
| Church/City: | Phone: |
| Funeral Home/City: | If prepaid, account #: | Phone: |
| Cemetery/City: | If purchased, what row #: | Lot #: | Block #: | Section #: |
| Casket or Urn Company: | If prepaid, account #: | Phone: |
| Preferred Clergy: | |
| Meal after funeral? Where? | |
| Memorial Service *(in another city?)*: | |
| Obituaries *(what cities?)*: | |
| Preferred Pall Bearers: | |
| Flowers? Or Memorials to?: | |
| Special Songs Requested: | |
| Special Scriptures: | |
| Special Poems or Stories: | |
| Preferred Singer/s: | |
| Preferred Instrumentalist/s: | |
| Preferred Speaker/s: | |
| Should gospel (&/or testimony) be shared? Invitation for salvation given? | |
| Instructions for choosing casket or urn: | |
| Clothing or jewelry desires: | |
| Grave marker choice: | |
| Location of Will, Policies, etc.: | |
| Viewing choice:  ■ Public Viewing   ■ Private family viewing only   ■ No viewing | |
| Burial/Cremation choice:  ■ Casket followed by burial   ■ Casket followed by cremation   ■ Cremation | |
| If casket, open or closed? | |
| If cremated what to do with ashes? | |
| Items for the memorial table: | |
| Location of photos *(computer files?)*: | |
| Other: | |

# PERSONAL INFORMATION & FUNERAL PLANS (Woman)

*Use additional paper if necessary*

| | |
|---|---|
| Full Name: | Social Security Number: |
| Date of Birth (DOB): | Place of Birth: |
| Driver's License State/Number: | |

Full Name of Father:            Father's Birthplace:            Father's DOB:
Full Name of Mother:            Mother's Birthplace:            Mother's DOB:
Siblings and their current location:

If married, Wedding Date:            Spouse's Maiden Name:            DOB:
Child #1 Name:            DOB:        Soc Sec #:            Spouse:
Child #2 Name:            DOB:        Soc Sec #:            Spouse:
Child #3 Name:            DOB:        Soc Sec #:            Spouse:
Child #4 Name:            DOB:        Soc Sec #:            Spouse:
Occupations/Position -Title/Years:
Employers/Years:
Do you have any life insurance with an Accidental Death Benefit *(which pays extra if you died accidentally)*?
Grade School/s, Middle School/Jr. Highs/Cities:
High School(s)/City/Year Graduated:
College(s)/Universities/Years/Cities/Degrees/Majors:
Places lived in/years:
Military from _____ to _____ in the (branch):        Rank:        Serial #:        Discharge Date:
Places served in Military:
Churches Attended/Cities/Years:
Professional Groups, Civic, Clubs, Lodges, Associations:
Closest friends:

## FUNERAL PLANNING *Provide instructions, notes, name(s), addresses, phone numbers, emails, etc.*

Church/City:            Phone:
Funeral Home/City:            If prepaid, account #:            Phone:
Cemetery/City:            If purchased, what row #:        Lot #:        Block #:        Section #:
Casket or Urn Company:            If prepaid, account #:            Phone:
Preferred Clergy:
Meal after funeral? Where?
Memorial Service *(in another city?)*:
Obituaries *(what cities?)*:
Preferred Pall Bearers:
Flowers? Or Memorials to?:
Special Songs Requested:
Special Scriptures:
Special Poems or Stories:
Preferred Singer/s:
Preferred Instrumentalist/s:
Preferred Speaker/s:
Should gospel *(&/or testimony)* be shared?   Invitation for salvation given?
Instructions for choosing casket or urn:
Clothing or jewelry desires:
Grave marker choice:
Location of Will, Policies, etc.:
Viewing choice:  ■ Public Viewing   ■ Private family viewing only   ■ No viewing
Burial/Cremation choice:  ■ Casket followed by burial   ■ Casket followed by cremation   ■ Cremation
If casket, open or closed?
If cremated what to do with ashes?
Items for the memorial table:
Location of photos *(computer files?)*
Other:

# DISTRIBUTION OF SPECIAL PERSONAL POSSESSIONS

*To view filled out samples, go to: www.MyFamilyForms.org*

This form helps you consider leaving specific personal items to specific people or ministries – your children, grandchildren, relatives, special friends, colleagues, church, Christian workers, ministries, charities, etc.
Items to be considered could include:

- Special collections
- Jewelry
- Instruments
- Certain articles of clothing
- Military paraphernalia
- Awards
- Artwork

- Handmade items
- Travel artifacts
- Family heirlooms
- Dishes
- Silverware
- Kitchenware
- Books

- Bibles
- Sports/Hunting/Recreation Entertainment equipment
- Electronics
- Furniture
- Vehicles
- Antiques

- Craft items
- Pictures or Photographs
- Tools
- _____
- _____
- _____

In the form below, write a description for the specific item, then put a "P" after the item if you have personally talked with the person about this item, and they know it has been promised to them. Put an "S" after the item if this gift will be a surprise to them. To be a legally binding document, it will be important to provide this information to the person who draws up your will or estate plans, so they can include this information as part of your official wishes.

| Description and Location of Item | Person/Relationship or Ministry/Organization | P or S |
|---|---|---|
| | | |

# EQUITABLE DISTRIBUTION OF FAMILY POSSESSIONS

*To view filled out samples, go to: www.MyFamilyForms.org*

After the distribution of Special Personal Possessions *(see previous form)*, there will usually be additional items that need to be distributed. Use this form to equitably distribute remaining possessions.

## Instructions:

A. Have one individual go through the remaining possessions and write down brief item descriptions *(Make additional copies of this form if necessary)*.

B. Make copies of this completed inventory and distribute to family members.

C. Allow everyone a specific time period (probably 24 or 48 hours) to fill out this sheet.

D. Have everyone put the following numbers by each item:
- 1=Would really like
- 2=Would be willing to take
- 3=No interest

E. Then have the executor of the estate, or a trusted family member, seek to equally and equitably divide up the number of #1's or #2's each family member receives. Distribute unwanted items to charity.

**Name(s) of family members:**

| Item Description | Choice # | Item Description | Choice # | Item Description | Choice # |
|---|---|---|---|---|---|
| 1 | | 24 | | 47 | |
| 2 | | 25 | | 48 | |
| 3 | | 26 | | 49 | |
| 4 | | 27 | | 50 | |
| 5 | | 28 | | 51 | |
| 6 | | 29 | | 52 | |
| 7 | | 30 | | 53 | |
| 8 | | 31 | | 54 | |
| 9 | | 32 | | 55 | |
| 10 | | 33 | | 56 | |
| 11 | | 34 | | 57 | |
| 12 | | 35 | | 58 | |
| 13 | | 35 | | 59 | |
| 14 | | 37 | | 60 | |
| 15 | | 38 | | 61 | |
| 16 | | 39 | | 62 | |
| 17 | | 40 | | 63 | |
| 18 | | 41 | | 64 | |
| 19 | | 42 | | 65 | |
| 20 | | 43 | | 66 | |
| 21 | | 44 | | 67 | |
| 22 | | 45 | | 68 | |
| 23 | | 46 | | 69 | |

# PEOPLE AND GROUPS TO NOTIFY ABOUT MY HOMEGOING

**Suggestion:** It is often possible to have your family contact "one key person" who will contact/call someone and have them call others on your family's behalf (e.g. one well networked cousin can contact all of our other cousins).

LOCATION OF MY ADDRESS BOOK: _____.

**Potential people or groups to be notified of your homegoing could include:**

- Parents
- Grandparents
- Siblings
- Cousins
- Aunts-Uncles
- Nieces-Nephews
- Children
- Grandchildren
- Great Grandchildren
- Employers
- Sports friends
- Work friends
- Childhood friends
- School friends
- Hobby friends
- Churches
- Civic Groups/Clubs
- Fraternal Organizations
- Professional Organizations/Associations
- Professional journals/magazines/newsletters
- Alumni magazines
- Current town/city Newspapers
- Past town/city Newspapers

Notice of my home going, funeral plans, and/or copies of my obituary should be sent to the following:

| Person's name, Group, or Newspaper | Telephone or Email or Address | Relationship | Who should they tell about my death |
|---|---|---|---|
| | | | |
| | | | |
| | | | |
| | | | |
| | | | |
| | | | |
| | | | |
| | | | |
| | | | |
| | | | |
| | | | |
| | | | |
| | | | |
| | | | |
| | | | |
| | | | |
| | | | |
| | | | |
| | | | |
| | | | |
| | | | |

# 40+ THINGS TO DO AFTER A LOVED ONE DIES

| Date | Items a Spouse, Family Member(s) or Executor Needs to Review and Act Upon *(As Applicable)* |
|---|---|
| | 1. Make sure the person's organ donation wishes are followed. |
| | 2. Contact funeral home *(if applicable, have prepaid funeral plans or life insurance information available)*. |
| | 3. Contact clergy and/or church. |
| | 4. Locate address book and notify family and friends *(by phone and/or e-mail)*. |
| | 5. Place obituary(s). |
| | 6. Contact Veterans Administration *(Military honors for funeral and death benefits)*. www.va.gov |
| | 7. Conduct viewing and/or service(s). |
| | 8. Order an adequate number of death certificates from the funeral home *(at least 10-15)*. |
| | 9. Locate will, trusts, important papers/documents/statements/memos/deeds/titles. |
| | 10. Review will, trust, estate, and probate information with executor and/or attorney *(identify attorney fees)*. |
| | 11. Distribute personal possessions *(as recorded in this booklet, will, or estate papers)*. |
| | 12. Write thank you notes for food, flowers, memorials, people who assisted in the service(s), etc. |
| | 13. Notify employer or employer's HR department *(apply for any life insurance benefits, pension benefits, transfer any medical coverage into the name of the spouse)*. |
| | 14. Notify life insurance companies and apply for benefits. |
| | 15. Gather unpaid bills you find or that come in the mail. Organize the information for payment from the estate. |
| | 16. Notify the Social Security Department and apply for benefits. 1-800-772-1213 www.ssa.gov |
| | 17. Notify company(s) holding pension account(s) and apply for benefits. |
| | 18. Notify any provider of income source(s) about the person's death. |
| | 19. Notify company(s) holding annuity account(s). |
| | 20. Notify the motor vehicle department and change titles for vehicles, boats, recreation vehicles. |
| | 21. Notify stock brokerage houses and investment companies where the person had accounts. |
| | 22. Notify motor vehicle departments. |
| | 23. Notify the post office. |
| | 24. Notify credit card companies *(apply for any possible life insurance benefits that might exist on the account)*. |
| | 25. Notify bank(s) or credit union(s) and change account information. |
| | 26. If applicable, reestablish title/ownership of Safe Deposit Box. |
| | 27. Change all jointly held accounts, investments, mortgages. |
| | 28. Get help going through a person's personal belongings—identify items you will keep, items you will give away to specific individuals, and items you will donate or have picked up (by a church, Christian organization or a local charity) for their use or resale. |
| | 29. Distribute any memorial gifts or charitable gifts to church, ministries, missionaries or non-profit organizations. |
| | 30. If applicable, apply for Veterans Administration benefits. www.va.gov |
| | 31. Review bank records and cancel automatic withdrawals related specifically to the deceased. |
| | 32. Notify any union, professional, religious, or fraternal organizations or associations to which the person belonged. Some groups will announce this to their membership. Also, check to see if there are any life insurance benefits the person may have had through their membership in these groups. |
| | 33. Review mail and cancel subscriptions and reoccurring charges *(cell phone, etc.)*. |
| | 34. Contact Medicare for possible assistance with the final medical bills, if the person was 65 or over. |
| | 35. Finalize hospital bills, doctor bills, nursing home accounts. |
| | 36. Notify any creditors and mortgage companies *(Note: See if any loans were insured. For example, the person may have had a home owner's insurance policy that pays off the mortgage at their death)*. |
| | 37. Locate previous tax records. File federal and state taxes for the year the person passed away. |
| | 38. Have executor transfer assets and inheritances to heirs and beneficiaries. |
| | 39. If applicable, become part of a grief support group or identify someone(s) who can journey with you through the grieving and adjustment process. |
| | 40. Have an autoresponder setup on a person's e-mail address. After several months, delete e-mail address. |
| | 41. Give charitable gifts or establish scholarship accounts in loving memory of the person that passed away. |
| | 42. Distribute any pictures, personal mementos, family heritage/legacy information to family, relatives, friends. |
| | 43. Research if there is any unclaimed money sitting in insurance companies, banks, utility companies, stocks, etc., go to: www.missingmoney.com |

# TOP 10 ESTATE PLANNING MISTAKES

Here is a "Top 10 List" pertaining to an important topic—will and estate planning. This list may start you thinking about your estate plan. Perhaps you're making one or more of the following mistakes:

1. **Thinking you don't need an estate plan:** No estate is too small, and you're never too young to have an estate plan. This lets your loved ones know how you want your assets distributed. Every adult, regardless of age, should have an estate plan.
2. **Putting off writing or updating your will:** Later may be too late. It is especially important for families with minor children to have a will specifying legal guardians and trustees.
3. **Having a will as your total estate plan:** There are other important parts to an estate plan besides a will. Many of the forms in this Legacy Organizer will be vital to your family's welfare.
4. **Underestimating the size of your estate:** Your estate is probably worth more than you think. Have you considered life insurance, appreciated value of your home and property, potential inheritances, retirement plans, etc.? Accurate values make a big difference in estate tax planning.
5. **Leaving your entire estate to your spouse or having all assets in joint ownership with your spouse:** For some this may be a good plan, for others it might be the wrong thing to do. Poor planning can result in substantial and unnecessary federal estate taxes or probate expense upon the death of the surviving spouse.
6. **Not understanding estate taxes:** Estate taxes may be considerably reduced or avoided with proper planning.
7. **Not using the annual gift tax exclusion:** This is a good way to enjoy sharing your estate with loved ones and individuals now. It may also help reduce future estate taxes. As of 2008 you can give $12,000/person.
8. **Keeping life insurance in your estate:** Life insurance will be considered part of your taxable estate unless you take steps to avoid this potential estate tax liability.
9. **Failing to keep good records:** All of your financial assets, accounts, wills, trusts, capital improvements, insurance policies, etc., should be up-to-date and easy to find. You should tell someone you trust where to find these important records.
10. **Failing to name your church, Christian ministries, or charities in your estate plan:** Have you considered leaving part of your estate to God's work? The government supports your decision to include Christian causes in your estate plan, and such gifts can help reduce your taxes now and later.

Source: Dick Edic of www.VisionResourcingGroup.com Used by permission.

*There are only three places to distribute your estate: family/friends, ministry/charity, or the government. If you don't do some basic planning, the government may get more than you ever intended, your family may be left confused, angry or short-changed, and God's work will get nothing.*

## WHEN should you consider changing or updating your existing will, trust, living will, estate, or charitable giving plans?

- You need to change your estate executor, personal representative, power of attorney, or medical power of attorney because you have changed your mind, the person has died, or the selected person cannot fulfill this role.
- Additional children have been born or adopted, or your choice(s) of guardians has changed for underage children.
- You want to restate your end-of-this-life medical preferences and wishes.
- You have moved to a different state or have purchased real estate in a different state.
- Your financial affairs and assets have changed.
- You desire to make a specific or significant charitable gift to a church, ministry, or non-profit organization.
- A beneficiary has died.
- Tax laws have changed that will impact your estate.
- Professional advisors have shown you ways to restructure your estate plans to decrease your tax liability and increase the amount you can leave to children, church, Christian ministries, or charities.
- Your attorney, accountant, or estate planner has advised you that changes are necessary.
- Your spouse has died, or you have become divorced.
- You want to include additional individuals in your estate plans (i.e., new grandchildren or great grandchildren).
- You want to change (add, delete, modify) how much a specific individual, church, ministry, or charity receives.

# TOP 5 WAYS TO GET YOUR HOUSE IN ORDER

## Facing Fundamental Issues Regarding Your Faith, Final Wishes, Finances, Family & Funeral

**To listen to this message by Internet, MP3, or as a Podcast, go to: www.MyFamilyForms.org**

*"This is what the LORD says: Put your house in order, because you are going to die."* Isaiah 38:1

### 1. Get your faith in order

- **Eccl. 9:12** *No man knows when his hour will come.*
- **Heb. 9:27** *It is destined that each person dies only once and after that comes judgment.* ᴺᴸᵀ
- **2 Cor. 5:10** *We (Christ following believers) must all appear before the judgment seat of Christ, that each one may receive what is due him for the things done while in the body, whether good or bad.*
- **1 John 5:11-13** *This is the testimony: God has given us eternal life, and this life is in his Son. He who has the Son has life; he who does not have the Son of God does not have life. I write these things to you who believe in the name of the Son of God so that you may KNOW hat you have eternal life.*
- **John 3:3** *Jesus declared, "I tell you the truth, no one can see the kingdom of God unless he is born again."*

### 2. Get your final wishes in order (medical/health care directives)

- **Prov. 27:12** *A sensible man watches for problems ahead and prepares to meet them. The simpleton never looks and suffers the consequences.* ᵀᴸᴮ
- **2 Cor. 5:1-4** *We know that when this tent we live in now is taken down-when we die and leave these bodies-we will have wonderful new bodies in heaven, homes that will be ours forever-more, made for us by God himself and not by human hands. How weary we grow of our present bodies. That is why we look forward eagerly to the day when we shall have heavenly bodies that we shall put on like new clothes. For we shall not be merely spirits without bodies. These earthly bodies make us groan and sigh.* ᵀᴸᴮ

### 3. Get your finances in order

- **Prov. 27:23-24** *Riches can disappear fast. And the king's crown doesn't stay in his family forever-so watch your business interests closely. Know the state of your flocks and your herds.* ᵀᴸᴮ
- **Prov. 3:9** *Honor the Lord with your capital (wealth, riches, goods, possessions, substance) and sufficiency from righteous labors and with the first fruits of all your income (revenues, increase, fruit, produce).* ᴬᴹᴾ
- **Deut. 16:17** *Each of you must bring a gift in proportion to the way the LORD your God has blessed you.*

### 4. Get your family affairs in order

- **Prov. 13:22** *A good man leaves an inheritance for his children's children.*
- **Prov. 20:21** *An inheritance quickly gained at the beginning will not be blessed at the end.* (See also: Luke 15:11-24 Prodigal son).
- **Prov. 17:16** *What use is money in the hand of a fool, since he has no desire to get wisdom?*
- **Prov. 19:14** *Houses (=a place to live) and wealth (=enough stuff for the place you live) are inherited from parents, but a prudent wife is from the LORD.*

### 5. Get your funeral celebration in order

- **1 Thess. 4:13-14** *Brothers, we do not want you to be ignorant about those who fall asleep, or to grieve like the rest of men, who have no hope. We believe that Jesus died and rose again and so we believe that God will bring with Jesus those who have fallen asleep in him.*

The rest of this manual provides helpful Biblical insights, practical ideas, and helpful forms to better communicate your medical wishes (health care directives), financial information, life legacy, Biblical generosity, and funeral planning desires with loved ones and professionals.

# 9 BIBLICAL INSIGHTS FOR END-OF-THIS-LIFE PLANNING

### 1. Recognize the certainty of your departure from this world and the need to get your house in order
- **Isaiah 38:1** This is what the LORD says: "Put your house in order, because you are going to die." Also look up: Eccl. 5:15, Prov. 27:12, Eccl. 9:12, Ps. 39:5-6, Eccl. 5:19-20, Eccl. 4:7-8, Eccl. 6:1-2.

### 2. Recognize the certainty of judgment to come and the opportunity for eternal life vs. eternal punishment
- **Heb. 9:27** It is destined that each person dies only once and after that comes judgment. NLT
- **2 Cor. 5:10** We (Christ following believers) must all appear before the judgment seat of Christ, that each one may receive what is due him for the things done while in the body, whether good or bad.
- **1 John 5:11-13** This is the testimony: God has given us eternal life, and this life is in his Son. He who has the Son has life; he who does not have the Son of God does not have life. I write these things to you who believe in the name of the Son of God so that you may know that you have eternal life.

### 3. Recognize the need to honor the Lord from whatever resources He has entrusted to you while you are living AND when you are leaving this earth (i.e., legacy giving)
- **Deut. 8:17-18** You may say to yourself, "My power and the strength of my hands have produced this wealth for me." But remember the LORD your God, for it is he who gives you the ability to produce wealth.
- **Prov. 3:9** Honor the Lord with your capital (wealth, riches, goods, possessions, substance) and sufficiency from righteous labors and with the first fruits of all your income (revenues, increase, fruit, produce). AMP
- **Deut. 16:17** Each of you must bring a gift in proportion to the way the LORD your God has blessed you.

RECOMMENDATION: **Remember your church, Christian ministries, and/or missionaries and charitable interests in your will.**

IMPORTANT NOTE: Many standardized attorney or will forms do NOT ask about your Christian or charitable interests. This is something you must personally and intentionally insert into your will.
**Here is sample wording from our estate plans:**
"Seven months after our death, the financial net assets are to be distributed as follows:
10% to our current local church
5% to Fort Wilderness Ministries in McNaughton, WI
3% to Samaritan's Purse in Boone, NC
2% to Gospel for Asia in Plano, TX
Remainder to be distributed as instructed or to be put into trust(s) for our children."

### 4. Be aware of the pitfalls of giving an inheritance all at once (at death or before death)
- **Prov. 20:21** An inheritance quickly gained at the beginning will not be blessed at the end.
- **Luke 15:11-24** The story of the prodigal son and his demanding an earlier inheritance.

SUGGESTION: **Divide up inheritance distributions over three (3) or more time periods.**
**Here is sample wording from our estate plans:**
"Estate distributions to our children: 10% at age 23, 30% at age 27 and 60% at age 31. From each child's portion of the estate, the trustee is to allow for monthly living, education, activities, and medical expenses for each child until they are 23. Each child is to go to their choice of a Torchbearer's Bible College for 1 year following their high school graduation before receiving funding towards their college education, vocational training, or business endeavors."

### 5. Consider wealth sharing before your death for special purposes
- **Prov. 19:14** Houses (a place to live) and wealth (enough stuff for the place you live) are inherited from parents, but a prudent wife is from the LORD.
- **Prov. 13:22** A good man leaves an inheritance for his children's children.

**Possible ideas** for "early inheritance gifts" for children or grandchildren could include: funds for education, vocational training, help in establishing a business, equipment, house down payment, household furnishings, music or athletic lessons, adoption, etc. According to current IRS rules, you're allowed to give $12,000 tax-free to any person or child each year.

### 6. Be wise when distributing wealth or estate resources

- **Prov. 17:16** What use is money in the hand of a fool, since he has no desire to get wisdom?
- **Prov. 17:2** A wise servant will rule over a disgraceful son, and will share the inheritance as one of the brothers.
- **Job 42:15** Nowhere in all the land were there found women as beautiful as Job's daughters, and their father granted them an inheritance along with their brothers.
- **Luke 9:25** What profit is it to a man if he gains the whole world, and is himself destroyed or lost? NKJV

### 7. Be wise in naming guardians for minor children. Choose people that will honor your Christian beliefs and values

- **Prov. 22:6** Train a child in the way he should go, and when he is old he will not turn from it.
- **Deut. 6:6-9** These commandments that I give you today are to be upon your hearts. Impress them on your children. Talk about them when you sit at home and when you walk along the road, when you lie down and when you get up. Tie them as symbols on your hands and bind them on your foreheads. Write them on the door frames of your houses and on your gates.

### 8. Research and receive professional counsel on appropriate legal ways to lay up for yourselves more treasure in heaven *(i.e. limit funds going to taxes and redirect these resources to God's work on earth)*

- **Matt. 6:19-21** (Jesus said) "Do not store up for yourselves treasures on earth, where moth and rust destroy, and where thieves break in and steal. But store up for yourselves treasures in heaven, where moth and rust do not destroy, and where thieves do not break in and steal. For where your treasure is, there your heart will be also."
- **1 Tim. 6:17-19** Command those who are rich in this present world not to be arrogant nor to put their hope in wealth, which is so uncertain, but to put their hope in God, who richly provides us with everything for our enjoyment. Command them to do good, to be rich in good deeds, and to be generous and willing to share. In this way they will lay up treasure for themselves as a firm foundation for the coming age, so that they may take hold of the life that is truly life.

### 9. Be wise in your distribution of personal possessions

- **Prov 27:12** A sensible man watches for problems ahead and prepares to meet them. The simpleton never looks and suffers the consequences. TLB

On pages 35 and 36 of this booklet, you will find forms which will allow you to provide a clear and equitable distribution of your personal possessions. When your personal possessions are distributed after your death, the following possible distribution levels can be used.

**Distribution 1:** Any items indicated on page 35 of this booklet are to be distributed.
**Distribution 2:** Each child is to fill out their list and return their form *(see page 36)* within 48 hours to the Personal Representative. The Personal Representative will then seek to, as much as possible, fairly distribute the personal property.
**Distribution 3:** A similar list of remaining items can then be given to *(indicate names of specific relatives or friends.)*
**Distribution 4:** Any remaining assets are to be sold and/or given to local charities *(i.e., ARC, Salvation Army, or Goodwill)*.

# GUARDIAN CHOICES FOR CHILDREN

*To view filled out samples, go to: www.MyFamilyForms.org*

One of the most important decisions you need to make concerning your under-age children is who will become their guardian if you were to die before they were 18. Even after 18 years old, it is still important to designate someone who can help provide godly counsel, wisdom, prayer, and care for their life and their choices.

It will be helpful to consider each child individually, as well as the family unit, when it comes to guardianship issues. It is usually best to appoint a few choices in order of your preference, in case a desired guardian is unavailable or unable to serve in this important role.

In addition to family considerations, it is important to identify potential guardians who share similar spiritual and personal beliefs.

**Name of Child:**     **Date of Birth:**     **Soc Sec #:**

| Likes & Dislikes: | Special notes: | Wishes for future activities/experiences: | Your hopes/dreams for their future: |
|---|---|---|---|
| | | | |

1st Choice - Name(s):     Location:
Email:     Phone:     Relationship:

2nd Choice - Name(s):     Location:
Email:     Phone:     Relationship:

3rd Choice - Name(s):     Location:
Email:     Phone:     Relationship:

**Name of Child:**     **Date of Birth:**     **Soc Sec #:**

| Likes & Dislikes: | Special notes: | Wishes for future activities/experiences: | Your hopes/dreams for their future: |
|---|---|---|---|
| | | | |

1st Choice - Name(s):     Location:
Email:     Phone:     Relationship:

2nd Choice - Name(s):     Location:
Email:     Phone:     Relationship:

3rd Choice - Name(s):     Location:
Email:     Phone:     Relationship:

**Name of Child:**     **Date of Birth:**     **Soc Sec #:**

| Likes & Dislikes: | Special notes: | Wishes for future activities/experiences: | Your hopes/dreams for their future: |
|---|---|---|---|
| | | | |

1st Choice - Name(s):     Location:
Email:     Phone:     Relationship:

2nd Choice - Name(s):     Location:
Email:     Phone:     Relationship:

3rd Choice - Name(s):     Location:
Email:     Phone:     Relationship:

# HELPFUL IDEAS FOR A FAMILY MEETING

In the Bible, when people were nearing the end of this life they often gathered their family members around them and communicated important information with them.

If you effectively use many of the forms and lists in this *LEGACY ORGANIZER*, you will be in a wonderful position to clearly communicate a great deal of valuable information and important instructions to your spouse and loved ones. The best way to normally do this is to schedule a special evening, weekend retreat, or even a family vacation to gather family together and share important information everyone needs to know and understand. Without some type of clear verbal and written communications, family members often find themselves confused, upset, and hurt about things that happen in the closing months and the months following the death of a parent.

NOTE: Sometimes a family meeting is called and organized by the aging parents for their adult children (and possibly spouses and older grandchildren). Other times it is the adult children that come to the realization that they need to schedule a time to meet with their aging parent(s) to go over a number of important items together. On occasion, some families even decide to utilize outside professional counsel or a trusted family friend to help plan and guide a family meeting.

## Suggestions for the type of things that could be covered or included in one or more family meetings:

1. Take turns to express love and appreciation for each other.
2. Recall and share positive stories or life changing memories/moments with each other.
3. Reflect on the character qualities, personal attributes, and positive strengths of each other.
4. Ask or answer some key questions from the *LEGACY ORGANIZER* 100 questions *(see pages 1-4)*.
5. Identify and ask for forgiveness for any specific wrongs that have been done in the past.
6. Have the parent(s) express their wishes for their children's and grandchildren's futures.
7. Talk about future housing plans/needs and timing *(i.e. transitioning from a house to an apartment/townhome/condo, retirement community, living with adult children or sibling, assisted living, etc.)* and transportation plans (when it will be necessary to stop driving, who can help drive to appointments, etc.).
8. Talk about who *(adult child? adult children? sibling? relative? paid worker? assisted living staff?)* will assist with caregiving needs that arise in the future.
9. Review and discuss in detail the financial picture -- current and future *(see pages 13-18)*. Decide who will have power of attorney, access to financial accounts, and/or check writing authority.
10. Go over health insurance coverage and end of life medical wishes *(see page 21)*.
11. Go over spiritual issues related to the future *(see page 22)*.
12. Share with your family when and how you became a Christian, what Christ means to you, and your assurance that you know where you are going when you leave this earth. Express your desire for each of them to also come to have a personal faith in Christ.
13. Share and discuss funeral plans and wishes *(see pages 23-27)*.
14. If applicable, family business issues and planning for the future.
15. Share key aspects of the estate plans: Christian/charitable giving decisions and wishes, how will the estate finances be handled and divided up, who is the executor or trustee (why?), specific instructions on how assets and possessions are to be handled and divided up, where are key documents located, and any other questions.
16. Determine if there is a specific family member that can assist in helping to fill out many of the helpful forms associated with the *LEGACY ORGANIZER*.
17. Pray together. Sing a favorite hymn together.

*Some of these helpful ideas were provided by investment and family advisor, T. Randall Fairfax of* www.highlandusa.net

# ESTATE PLANNING TOOLS FOR EFFECTIVE CHRISTIAN & CHARITABLE GIVING

Adapted from materials by Dick Edic of www.VisionResourcingGroup.com

In 2 Kings 20:1, the prophet Isaiah went to King Hezekiah and said, *"Put your house in order, because you are going to die; you will not recover."* Basically, God was telling Hezekiah to complete his estate planning, so that when he died, his wishes could be carried out by those who survived him. Proverbs 13:22 says, *"A good man leaves an inheritance for his children's children"*. Estate planning is the process of planning your estate in such a way that after you die, it properly affects the people in your life, transfers your property efficiently while minimizing probate and tax expense, and guides those who will assist you in achieving your goals. It involves the right legal documents that will direct those in the process of settling your estate. Included in this process is the opportunity to leave a charitable gift. This is the sacred privilege given us by God to continue giving to His kingdom ministries after we are gone.
**Here is a list of helpful tools for giving gifts from your current assets or estate plans.**

**Bequests** A bequest through a will or trust is the most common type of planned gift. Almost every adult should have a will or living trust, and every Christian should at least consider making gifts to their church, ministries, and favorite charities through his or her estate. Since everything a person owns (during life and at death) belongs to God, a Christian should distribute the estate to family members, friends, and ministries that will use those assets in a way that honors the Lord. A gift through a will or trust can be a specified dollar amount or a percentage of the estate. Since the final size of the estate is uncertain at the time the will is written, it is often more desirable to use percentages than dollar amounts to describe how the estate is to be distributed. One of the benefits of a will or trust is that it can be changed at any time. A person can reevaluate his or her giving priorities as family and financial circumstances change over time. Any gift through a will or trust to a qualified charity is deductible for Federal Estate Tax purposes.

**Life Estate Gift** A person may deed a personal residence, farm, or other real property to the Lord's work now, but retain lifetime enjoyment and use of the property. The person may continue to live in the home. In the case of other property, the person may continue to collect any income generated. The person continues to pay the taxes, insurance, and maintenance of the property. At the person's death, the property becomes the immediate property of the church, ministry, or charity. If desired, the church or ministry may sell the property and use the cash proceeds. In the case of a personal residence, the church or ministry may decide to keep the home for use by pastoral staff or visiting missionaries, or ministry expansion. An irrevocable Life Estate Gift will generate a tax-deductible gift based on the "remainder interest" the person holds in the property. This value is determined according to government tables and the person's age. This amount may be claimed as a deduction for Federal Income Tax purposes in the year the agreement is completed. This arrangement removes the property from the estate, and it will not be subject to either probate or the Federal Estate Tax.

**Life Insurance Gifts** Life insurance is one way of making a larger gift than a person may be able to make otherwise. This gift option is available for both new and existing policies. If done properly, the annual premiums paid on the policy can be deducted as a charitable gift for Federal Income Tax purposes. Life insurance proceeds are included in the gross estate for calculation of the Federal Estate Tax. If the beneficiary of the policy is a qualified charity, there is a charitable deduction for purposes of the Federal Estate Tax. Sometimes people have old life insurance policies they no longer need. They may be paid-up policies with significant cash value. These policies can be gifted directly to a church or ministry, who in turn can decide whether to cash them out or wait until it receives the death benefits. Another option is to encourage people to add their church or a ministry as one of the beneficiaries of an existing policy. Some people also choose to use the concept of "tithing" their life insurance proceeds just like in their will or living trust. They do this by changing their beneficiary designations.

**Charitable Remainder Unitrust** is designed for the person who wants to make a gift to the Lord's work, but needs income during life. This trust is especially suited for a person with highly appreciated property (either securities or real estate). It is possible to transfer the property to the trust and avoid all tax on capital gain. A Federal Income Tax deduction is available for the year the trust is created. It is based on the value of the trust, the age of the person, and the payout percentage selected. A Charitable Remainder Unitrust may be created and funded at the time of death for the benefit of one or more survivors. Assets transferred to the trust would not be subject to probate or the Federal Estate Tax. One or more Christian or charitable beneficiaries may be named in the trust. At the death of the person, the assets from the trust would be distributed to these charities. The Charitable Remainder Unitrust is one of the most technical gift plans, and requires expert help to both set up and manage. Your church's denominational foundation or independent counsel should be able to assist from the beginning to the end of this process.

**Charitable Lead Trust** is almost the opposite of the Charitable Remainder Unitrust. The person creates a trust to provide current income to a charitable organization for a specified period of time (5, 10, 15, or more years). At the end of that time the assets of the trust are returned to family members. The Charitable Lead Trust may help wealthy families transfer assets to heirs, with little or no estate or gift tax. Seek professional counsel.

**Gift Annuity Agreement - Deferred Gift Annuity Agreement** is a perfect plan for a person who wants to make a future gift and receive a guaranteed stream of income for life. Annuity rates are based on age, and often are quite competitive with what a person can earn from low risk investments in the market. A deferred payment annuity allows for payments to begin at a later day (such as at retirement), and results in both a larger charitable gift and a greater annual income. Both immediate and deferred annuity plans are an excellent means of "supplementing" retirement income, but are not meant to be retirement plans.

**Charitable Gift Annuity** is less complicated than a Charitable Remainder Unitrust (CRUT), but the CRUT has greater flexibility and applications. This plan provides a Federal Income Tax deduction in the year that the annuity is entered. The amount of the gift is determined by the age of the annuitant, the annuity rate, and the principal amount. Another advantage of the gift annuity is that part of the annual income is considered tax-exempt. Also, if the annuity is funded with appreciated securities, there is significant savings related to capital gains tax. A portion of the capital gain is avoided altogether, and the remainder is reported in small increments over the life expectancy of the annuitant. All remaining funds in the agreement at the annuitant's death are available for the ministries designated by the person. The amount placed in the annuity during life is removed from the estate and will not be subject to probate or the Federal Estate Tax. NOTE: The Gift Annuity Agreement and Deferred Gift Annuity Agreement are less complicated than the Charitable Remainder Trust. However, few churches or ministries would be able to administer their own annuity program. Again, refer to your denominational or independent counsel, or get help from the National Christian Community Foundation (www.NationalChristian.com 800-681-6223) in Atlanta, GA who can provide planned giving administration services.

**Living Trust** is a good "will substitute" estate-planning tool for some families. Such a trust can be written to include a charitable bequest, just like in a will. Assets in the trust are distributed according to the terms of the trust and do not pass through the probate process.

**Naming a church or ministry as a beneficiary** One easy method of making a planned gift is by naming the church, Christian ministry, or charity as beneficiary of any account that allows such a designation. A checking account or savings account would be one example. In a banking situation, this is often known as a Pay on Death (or POD) account. Some institutions may refer to this arrangement as Transfer on Death (or TOD). These arrangements allow for the assets to pass directly to the named beneficiary and avoid the probate process.

**Retirement plans** allow the owner to name a beneficiary, or beneficiaries. At the death of some high wealth individuals, there may be two taxes levied against a qualified or tax-deferred retirement account—income and estate. These taxes can be avoided if the "secondary" beneficiary of the plan is a qualified charity. This is "win-win" because family members would end up inheriting the same amount or more when using this tax strategy. With married couples, when a spouse dies, the "primary" beneficiary is usually the other spouse. The surviving spouse could then "roll" the tax-deferred retirement account into a personal tax-deferred retirement account and continue to defer any income taxes. When he or she dies and the proceeds of the account go to a "non-spouse," like children, that becomes a "taxable event." Current tax laws allow children to "stretch out" their receipt and subsequent taxation of the proceeds. However, by naming a church, ministry, or charity as the "secondary" beneficiary, some or all of potential income taxes can be avoided. Since other assets in the estate may not be subject to income taxes at death, such as cash, life insurance or real estate, consider "using" the tax-deferred retirement account for any charitable gifts and pass the other assets to children or friends.

**Automatic Transfers** at death are often referred to as "will substitutes" because they bypass distribution through the will. Such transfers avoid the probate process. These assets will avoid the Federal Estate Tax when transferred to a qualified charity. Examples are joint tenancy, life insurance, IRAs and business agreements.

**Endowment or Scholarship Funds** can be set up so that members can make current or deferred gifts into the endowment or scholarship fund knowing that it will annually give from the earnings of the investment portfolio in the fund. These funds can produce an economic "hedge" against hard times.

**Outright Gifts (other than cash)** Gifts other than cash can be a significant benefit to a local church or ministry. Such gifts might include stocks, bonds, mutual fund shares, real property, or tangible property. Transfer of ownership will often require some form of legal document. There are special Internal Revenue Service rules for valuing and reporting non-cash gifts. The tax-deductible value of some gifts will be limited to the person's cost basis or the Fair Market Value (whichever is lower). You will be allowed to deduct the full value of some gifts (including all appreciation), and will avoid any tax on capital gain. Any property given during life will be removed from the estate, and will not be subject to probate or the Federal Estate Tax.

# ADDITIONAL RESOURCES

## Resources for your personal finances

- Crown Financial Ministry: **www.Crown.org** or 800-722-1976
- Compass - Finances God's Way: **www.Compass1.org**
- Willow Creek Association's Good Sense Ministry: **www.GoodSenseMinistry.com**
- Dave Ramsey Radio Show: **www.DaveRamsey.com**
- **www.iQuestions.com** *Experts provide video answers to questions about life and finances*
- **www.360financialliteracy.org**

## Resources to help you become more generous

- **www.GenerosityPledge.org Movement** *30 day devotional on the 7 Keys to Open-Handed Living in a Tight-Fisted World*
- **www.GenerousLife.org** *Bestselling 40 Day Bible devotional to help people become more generous*
- **www.MAXIMUMgenerosity.org** *Generosity resources by Brian Kluth for use in churches and ministries*
- **www.GiveWithJoy.org** *Radio stories and free 40 Day eDevotional to inspire generosity*
- Generous Giving: **www.GenerousGiving.org**
- The Gathering: **www.TheGathering.com** *(for those giving over $200K/year)*
- National Christian Foundation: **www.NationalChristian.com** or 800-681-6223 *This organization can help you set up your own your own charitable giving account (donor advised funds).*
- **www.GenerousYou.com**

## Resources for investing

- Sound Mind Investing with Austin Pryor: **www.SoundMindInvesting.com**
- Stewardship Partners: **www.StewardshipPartners.com** *(for people with over $100K to invest)*

## Resources for financial & estate planning

- Because I Love You CHRISTIAN LEGACY ORGANIZER: **www.MyFamilyForms.org**
- Fulcrum Philanthropy Systems: **www. Fulcrumps.com**
- Kingdom Advisors: **www.KingdomAdvisors.org** or 404-497-7680
- Ron Blue & Company: **www.RonBlue.com** or 800-841-0362
- The Christian Legal Society: **www.CLSnet.org** *Referrals to Christ-centered attorneys.*

## Help with your giving and philanthropy

- Evangelical Council for Financial Accountability: **www.ecfa.org** or 800-3BE-WISE
- **www.GuideStar.org** *IRS990 financials for non-profits.*
- **www.NetworkforGood.org** *Allows you to give electronically to churches, ministries and non-profit charities.*
- **www.MinistryWatch.com**
- **www.iDonate.com** *Allows you to donate cars, property, and assets to your church or favorite charities.*
- Better Business Bureau for Charities: **www.Give.com**

## Help for Christian CEO's and business owners

- Fellowship of Companies for Christ International: **www.FCCI-online.org**
- **www.360financialliteracy.org**

# PRODUCTS AND RESOURCES BY DR. BRIAN KLUTH

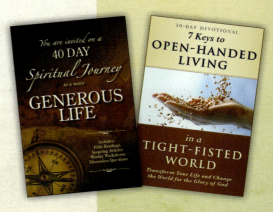

## GENEROSITY DEVOTIONALS FOR CHURCH-WIDE USE

*"40 Day Spiritual Journey to a More Generous Life"*
Preview digital copy or order at www.GenerousLife.org
(Over 450,000 copies & translations in over 40 foreign languages)

*30 Day Devotional: "7 Keys to Open-Handed Living in a Tight-Fisted World"*
Preview digital copy or order at www.GenerosityPledge.org

Brian's generosity devotionals, videos, and companion materials have been used by thousands of churches across America and around the world to inspire greater generosity and increase giving. Some church have even reported miraculous results when they have seen giving increases of 10%, 20%, 35%, 50%, 60%, 100%.

## BOOK, AUDIO TEACHING CD, AND BOOKMARK

*"Experience God as Your Provider: Finding Faith and Financial Stability in Unstable Times"*

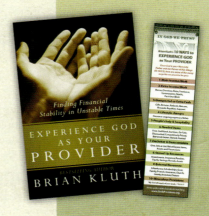

This material and teaching has revolutionized people's thinking and helped them understand that God is bigger than stock markets, job markets, and housing markets. Regardless of what is happening in the world's economy, God has many creative ways to care for people in the midst of challenging times. These materials are ideal for churches, Sunday School classes, small groups, or personal use. These resources make great appreciation gifts for ministries to give to their donors/supporters. Discounts are available for group or larger orders. *Go to:* www.GodIsYourProvider.com

## ONLINE GENEROSITY KITS or CD FOR CHURCHES
*Downloadable Internet Packages of Generosity Resources for Churches*

In these online Generosity Kits (or CD), pastors, leaders and committees will receive a smorgasbord of hundreds of dollars of generosity resources they can use to inspire greater generosity and increase giving. Packages run from $59 and up and include Power Point offertory slides, generosity cartoons, flyers, materials for church finance and stewardship committees, sermon helps, planning guides and worksheets, videos, *"best generosity practices"* of leading churches, and much more! To order or to preview, *go to:* www.MAXIMUMgenerosity.org

## MEDIA INTERVIEWS & GUEST SPEAKING

BRIAN KLUTH on CBN
Natl. & Intl. TV interview

Dr. Brian Kluth is recognized as a national media expert and speaker on end of life issues, giving trends in America, and generosity. He has been interviewed or his work has been featured by CNN, NBC, CBS, FOX, CBN, USA Today (front page), Washington Times (front page), National Public Radio, Wall Street Journal, Kipliners, Reuters, Christianity Today, Chronicle of Philanthropy, and hundreds of radio programs, newspapers, and magazines. Brian is also a frequent key note guest speaker at large churches, colleges, financial conferences, clergy gatherings, leadership conventions, and fundraising events. For video/audio clips of Dr. Kluth's speaking or being interviewed on TV/radio, *go to:* www.kluth.org

# ORDERING THE LEGACY ORGANIZER

## ORDER ONLINE AT: www.MyFamilyForms.org
## or CALL 866.935.5884 or 719.302.3383

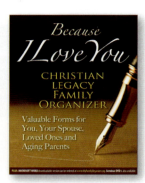

### PAPER VERSION
$29.95 for 1 copy
$19.95 each for 2 copies
$14.95 each for 3 to 9 copies
$9.95 each for 10 to 19 copies
$7.95 each for 20 to 49 copies
$4.95 each for 50 to 99 copies
$3.95 each for 100 to 299 copies
$2.95 each for *300 to 999 copies
$2.85 each for *1000 to 2499 copies
$2.75 each for *2500 to 15000 copies
CALL for *custom quote* for over 15,000 - 1-866-935-5884

*If you order 500 copies or more, you can customize the 4 page cover for just $1/more per copy. This is a great gift that will be used and appreciated for years to come!

### COMPUTER VERSION: MICROSOFT WORD & ADOBE PDF DIGITAL VERSION
For personal use, you can order the LEGACY ORGANIZER as a Microsoft Word and Adobe PDF version so you can print out pages OR customize any of the forms OR fill in the forms by computer (so you can edit and update the information as needed).

$19.95 each for 1 copy
$14.95 each for 2 copies
$9.95 each for 3 to 9 copies
$6.95 each for 10 to 49 copies
$4.95 each for 50 to 100 copies

 90 Minutes Seminar DVD *$10*

### COPYRIGHT REPRINT PERMISSION (Corporate / Church / Non Profit)
Receive a link to a webpage that will allow you to download an Adobe PDF file of the entire Legacy Organizer and PDF's of ALL the individual forms so you can print, photocopy, or post online to share with others

$99 to share with up to 50 people *(the entire Legacy Organizer OR any of the individual forms)*
$249 to share with up to 500 people ( " " )
$499 to share with up to 1000 people ( " " )
$799 to share with up to 2500 people ( " " )
$999 to share with up to 5000 people ( " " )
CALL for *custom quote* to share with over 10,000 people - 1-866-935-5884

### INDIVIDUAL FORMS FOR MEDIA INTERVIEWS & PUBLICATIONS
*For media interviews or articles, call Brian Kluth at 720.432.2422 (cell) or send an email to bk@kluth.org*
Brian Kluth is available for interviews for radio, TV, online, and print media. He also provides articles for print and online publications. Special arrangements can be made to make any of the individual forms available so they can appear in a printed publication or be posted online. Brian's financial work and research has been covered by CNN, NBC, FOX, CBS, ABC, Wall Street Journal, Washington Times (front page), Kiplingers, USA Today (front page), Associated Press Radio, NPR, and hundreds of radio stations and newspapers.

### COPYRIGHT PARTNERSHIP FOR CUSTOMIZED VERSIONS
*If you are interested in information or pricing for any of the following call* **1-866-935-5884**
**FULL CUSTOMIZED VERSIONS** are available to groups, organizations, companies, or churches that want to create their own customized version of the LEGACY ORGANIZER or any of the individual forms. Copyright permission is purchased (based on the quantity to be produced) that allows for full editing, adding, deleting or modifying any and all of the pages. Once an agreement is purchased, the LEGACY ORGANIZER'S InDesign software electronic files are provided to the purchaser. Printing can be done by their own printers or we can assist with providing a printing quote.

### NON-RELIGIOUS LEGACY VERSION AVAILABLE
For businesses, non-profits, groups, and financial professions that are interested in the legacy and end-of-life forms of our LEGACY ORGANIZER, there is a modified **non-religious** version available. Please go to **www.MyFamilyForms.org** for details.

> "In this LEGACY ORGANIZER I tried to create for you and your loved ones the most comprehensive collection of helpful family forms anywhere on the planet! I trust that any and every form you choose to fill out and use will help save hours, hassles, headaches, and heartache for you and the people you care about." — DR. BRIAN KLUTH

# TOP 10 TIPS
## on how to best use your LEGACY ORGANIZER

**1** Go to the www.MyFamilyForms.org website and listen to any of the available audio files or watch the videos to hear true stories that will inspire you on why and how to use many of the pages in this manual.

**2** Show or tell others about this helpful manual. Purchase paper or digital copies for family members, friends, clients, and others.

**3** Pick out a regular block of time each week for a few months (a morning, afternoon, or evening) to work on filling out pages that you know will be the most helpful to you, your spouse, and your loved ones.

**4** Write in pencil so you can later update or edit any information that changes.

**5** Bring the **LEGACY ORGANIZER** along to family gatherings (Christmas, Easter, Thanksgiving, family reunions, birthday parties, etc.) and have people discuss and fill out information on your family tree, 100 questions, birthdays and anniversaries, gift giving ideas, and more.

**6** If you have aging parents, have personal or family meeting(s) with them and help them fill out important information that is needed concerning their end of this life issues (especially the family tree and history section, financial information, medical wishes and history, funeral pages, distribution of possessions, spiritual matters, etc.).

**7** Organize a small group of people to meet together 4-8 times to work through the **LEGACY ORGANIZER** together and to hold each other accountable to keep making progress on filling out many of the key pages in this manual. The group could consist of people in your neighborhood, workplace (meet over the lunch hour), friends, family, church, Sunday School, Bible study, book group, and ladies group.

**8** Tell your church leaders, financial professionals, or non-proft organizations you support about this manual. Encourage them to order copies to give to their members, clients, or donors.

**9** Go to the www.MyFamilyForms.org website and order the electronic version so you can customize any page to fit you and your situation. You can also print out pages and put them in a 3-ring binder.

**10** Order the electronic version so you can update and edit the information and easily email it to family members in other places. Keep a file of this paper version or electronic document with your will.

## © COPYRIGHT RULES CONCERNING YOUR USE OF THE FORMS IN THIS LEGACY ORGANIZER

*All material in this LEGACY ORGANIZER has been developed through the personal experiences, work, and research of Dr. Brian Kluth. Once you have purchased a paper and/or electronic copy of the LEGACY ORGANIZER (or have been given a copy as a gift), you have permission to photocopy or print the forms in this manual for your personal use and to share your completed forms with others. If you want other family members and friends to have the blank forms found in this LEGACY ORGANIZER, please purchase a paper or electronic version for them or direct them to the www.MyFamilyForms.org website so they can make their own purchase. Photocopying, emailing, and/or distributing blank forms to others is not allowed. Copyright and reprint permission for specific forms is available upon request by emailing organizer@kluth.org with the details of how the form(s) will be used or modified and who will receive the forms (copyright fees may apply). Details and special pricing options for CUSTOM COVER copies and FULL CUSTOM VERSIONS (see page 39) are available upon request by calling 1-866-935-5884. Contact information: Dr. Brian Kluth, MAXIMUM Generosity, 9415 Wickerdale Ct. Highlands Ranch, CO 80130, organizer@kluth.org.*

© Dr. Brian Kluth. All rights reserved. Contents and blank forms may not be reproduced in whole or part in any form without the express written consent of the Author. DESIGNED BY: Leana Santana Scripture taken from the HOLY BIBLE®, NEW INTERNATIONAL VERSION. NIV® COPYRIGHT© 1973, 1978, 1984 by International Bible Society. Used by permission. All rights reserved. Any verses that are not NIV are designated as NLT (New Living Translation), TLB (Tyndale Living Bible), and KJV (King James Version). Holy Bible, New Living Translation, copyright © 1996 by Tyndale Charitable Trust. All rights reserved. Scripture quotations marked (NLT) are taken from the Holy Bible, New Living Translation, copyright © 1996. Used by permission of Tyndale House Publishers, Inc., Wheaton, Illinois 60189. All rights reserved. The Living Bible, copyright © 1971. Scripture quotations marked (TLB) are taken from the Living Bible. Used by permission of Tyndale House Publishers, Inc., Wheaton, Illinois 60189. All rights reserved. The two Scripture quotations marked (KJV) are taken from the King James Bible. Most photos were purchased from www.istockphotos.com. ISBN13: 978-1-4507-5272-5 Retail: $29.95US

# The Christian Legacy Organizer

## Your ULTIMATE GUIDE for organizing:

- ✓ Household Information
- ✓ Family History
- ✓ Important Records
- ✓ Finances
- ✓ Family Tree
- ✓ Password/Login Codes
- ✓ Will & Estate Plans
- ✓ Charitable Giving
- ✓ Important Faith Issues
- ✓ Care Giving (for Aging parents or Family Members)

## A GREAT GIFT idea for:

- ✓ Parents
- ✓ Clients
- ✓ Friends
- ✓ Donors
- ✓ Family
- ✓ Employees
- ✓ Aging Relatives
- ✓ Church or group members
- ✓ Selling in stores, salons, shops and waiting rooms

## About the Author and Speaker

**DR. BRIAN KLUTH** is a bestselling author, inspirational speaker, minister, and a leading media expert on end of life issues, giving in America, and generosity. He has been interviewed or his work has been featured by CNN, NBC, CBS, FOX, CBN, *USA Today*, *Washington Times*, National Public Radio, Wall Street Journal, Kipliners, Reuters, Christianity Today, Chronicle of Philanthropy, and hundreds of radio programs, newspapers, and magazines. Brian is also a frequent keynote speaker at large churches, colleges, financial conferences, clergy gatherings, leadership conventions, and fundraising events. Brian lives with his family in Denver, CO.